Meals, Music, and Muses

Also by the Authors

Between Harlem and Heaven: Afro-Asian-American Cooking for Big Nights, Weeknights, and Every Day by JJ Johnson and Alexander Smalls with Veronica Chambers

Grace the Table: Stories and Recipes from My Southern Revival by Alexander Smalls with Hettie Jones

Meals,
Music,

Recipes from My African American Kitchen

and Muses

Alexander Smalls

with Veronica Chambers

Food and Author Photography by Beatriz da Costa
Food Styling by Roscoe Betsill

FLATIRON
BOOKS
NEW YORK

www.flatironbooks.com

Grateful acknowledgment is made for permission to reproduce from the following:

"Quilting the Black-Eyed Pea (We're Going to Mars)" copyright © 2002 by Nikki Giovanni.

"Summertime" (from *Porgy and Bess*). Music and lyrics by George Gershwin, DuBose and Dorothy Heyward, and Ira Gershwin. Copyright © 1935 (renewed) Ira Gershwin Music, DuBose and Dorothy Heyward Memorial Fund, and George Gershwin Music. All rights for Ira Gershwin Music administered by WB Music Corp. All rights reserved. Used by permission of Alfred Music.

Ceramics courtesy of Margaret Braun and Luz Ceramics.

Photograph on pages ii–iii by Ancha Chiangmai/Shutterstock.com. Photograph on pages xvi–1 by Sean Pavone/Shutterstock.com. Photographs on pages 8–9, 28–29, 33, 56–57, 100–101, 115, 116–117, 154–155, and 174–175 by Shutterstock.com

Designed by SBI Book Arts

Endpapers designed by Jonathan Bush

The Library of Congress Cataloging-in-Publication Data is available upon request.

ISBN 978-1-250-09809-2 (paper over board)
ISBN 978-1-250-24100-9 (ebook)

Our books may be purchased in bulk for promotional, educational, or business use. Please contact your local bookseller or the Macmillan Corporate and Premium Sales Department at 1-800-221-7945, extension 5442, or by email at MacmillanSpecialMarkets@macmillan.com.

First Edition: February 2020

10 9 8 7 6 5 4 3 2 1

This book is dedicated to my parents . . . and my parents'
parents . . . and their parents. The ancestors . . . those whose silent
voices and extraordinary challenges shaped the world I inherited.
Their hardships . . . sacrifices made my life more meaningful
and promising . . . because of them I am . . . I stand on
their shoulders . . . Grateful . . . Thankful!

Contents

Introduction: Up South   1

1. Jazz
Starters

Deviled Eggs   12
Carolina Bourbon Barbecue Shrimp and Okra Skewers   15
   Carolina Bourbon Barbecue Sauce   *17*
Deviled Crab Cakes with Spicy Creole Mayonnaise   18
   Spicy Creole Mayonnaise   *21*
Hoppin' John Cakes with Sweet Pepper Rémoulade   22
   Sweet Pepper Rémoulade   *24*
Mustard-Barbecued Chicken Livers on Peppered Turnip Greens   25
   Mustard Barbecue Sauce   *27*

2. Spirituals
Rice, Pasta, and Grits: Comfort Things

Carolina Hoppin' John (Rice and Peas)   34
Charleston Spicy Red Rice   36
Gullah Dirty Rice   38

Savory Chicken Bog   41

Buttermilk Mac and Cheese   43

Dunbar Pie: Macaroni with Meat Sauce   46

Macaroni Vegetable Salad   48

Stone-Ground Grits   51

Grits and Sage Sausage Gravy   52

Smothered Shrimp and Crabmeat Pan Gravy   53

3. Gospel
Field Greens and Green Things

Carolina Cabbage Slaw with Roasted Sweet Corn   61

Field Greens, Poached Pear, and Black-Eyed Pea Salad with Citrus Vinaigrette   62

   Citrus Vinaigrette   65

Creole Caesar Salad with Corn Bread Croutons   67

   Creole Caesar Dressing   68

Spicy Okra Shrimp Soup   69

Fried Okra   70

Stewed Okra with Corn and Tomato   72

Roasted Okra with Herbs, Pepper, and Garlic   73

Broiled Sweet Corn with Tarragon-Cayenne Butter   75

Fried Sweet White Corn   76

Fresh Creamed Corn Garnished with Crispy Leeks   77

Corn Catfish Soup with Bacon and Mint   79

Sweet Pickle Potato Salad   80

Creole Potato Salad   83

Lemon Candied Yams   85

Citrus-Whipped Sweet Potatoes   86

Lady Lima Succotash Salad with Fresh Mint   87

Baked Spicy Barbecue Beans   90

Spicy Charleston Black Beans   91

Sautéed Green Beans with Toasted Charleston Benne Seeds   92

Stewed Collard Greens with Smoked Turkey   95

Pan-Fried Cabbage with Bacon   97

Herb-Sautéed Greens with Roasted Garlic and Turnips   98

4. Opera
Fish and Seafood

Fried Catfish Plate   104

Seared Grouper with Spicy Gumbo Sauce   107

   Spicy Gumbo Sauce   108

Shrimp and Okra Creole Sauté   109

Frogmore Stew   110

Sherry She-Crab Soup   113

5. Divas

Opening Night Dishes: Meat and Chicken

Roast Quail in Bourbon Cream Sauce   121

    Bourbon Cream Sauce   *123*

Free-Range Duck with Creole Sauce   124

    Creole Sauce   *126*

Oven-Fried Baby Chickens with Hot Mustard–Apricot Jam Glaze   127

    Hot Mustard–Apricot Jam Glaze   *129*

Southern Fried Chicken Plate   131

Alexander's "Chase the Blues Away" Hot Dogs   134

Roasted Stuffed Turkey with Corn Bread–Chestnut Dressing   136

    Corn Bread–Chestnut Dressing   *137*

Pan-Fried Rabbit with Root Vegetables and Redeye Gravy   139

Marinated Venison Roast with Ginger-Berry Glaze   141

    Ginger-Berry Glaze   *143*

Citrus-Glazed Pork Loin Roast with Corn Cream Sauce   144

    Corn Cream Sauce   *145*

Bourbon Praline Candied Baked Ham   146

    Bourbon Praline Sauce   *148*

Prime Rib Roast with Crawfish Onion Gravy   149

    Crawfish Onion Gravy   *150*

Braised Oxtails, Turnips, and Okra   151

6. Jukebox Music
Bread, Biscuits, and Muffins

Buttermilk Corn Bread Muffins   158
Buttermilk Biscuits   159
Sweet Potato Biscuits   162
Jam Biscuits   164
Sage Sausage Biscuits   166
Jalapeño Cheddar Biscuits   168
Sweet Potato Muffins   170
Angel Yeast Rolls   173

7. Serenades
Cakes, Pies, and Puddings

Sticky Buns   178
Doughnuts   180
Icebox Lemon Pie   183
Bourbon Pecan Pie   185
   Pie Shell   *186*
Chess Pie   187

Banana Pudding Custard Pie   188

Sweet Potato Pie   190

Carolina Rice Pudding   193

Blackberry Cobbler   194

Southern Pound Cake   197

Southern Comfort Peach Shortcake   200

Chocolate Pineapple Upside-Down Cake   202

Sweet Potato Coconut Cake   204

Bourbon Chocolate Praline Truffles   206

Acknowledgments   210

Appendix: Chapter Playlists   213

Index   217

Meals, Music, and Muses

Up
South

The Meals and Music That Are My American History

At my house, when entertaining, I overcook purposely. Most everyone leaves with a to-go bag. After a night at the theater or a musical concert, I like to plan a light late supper for friends. Something I can cook ahead and simply serve in less than thirty minutes—easy and understated like my Carolina Bourbon Barbecue Shrimp and Okra Skewers (page 15) or my Field Greens, Poached Pear, and Black-Eyed Pea Salad with Citrus Vinaigrette (page 62).

One friend, a frequent guest at my home, keeps me on my toes—always making sure there are plenty of vegetarian options. As I clear the table, he settles in at the piano and the music starts flowing. This is often how the after-party gets going at my house: it just takes one guest to find the piano, and the good times are *on*.

While I stack trays of my Bourbon Chocolate Praline Truffles (page 206) and ready the brandy glasses for bourbon and single malts, I enter the room to a chorus of tunes already being pursued. One particular night, the guest list included opera singers and Harlem neighbors, Broadway stars and pals who are legends only in their own minds. You don't have to be a professional singer, or even on pitch, to gather round a family piano and sing.

I joined in, leading the group of balladeers. We sang one fun hit after another, well into the night. Music and friends, chocolate and bourbon. I never have to leave the house to trip the lights fantastic.

In the United States, food and music are inextricably linked, especially in the African American culture. Both Southern music and Southern food are rooted in a knotty lineage that connects West Africa and Western Europe. "Food, music, and love are bound up in interesting, often humorous ways in the Southern vernacular," notes the Smithsonian Folkways Project. The longest running daily radio show in America is the *King Biscuit Hour*, out of Helena, Arkansas. The show got its name from its first sponsor, King Biscuit Flour. In turn,

In the United States, food and music are inextricably linked, especially in the African American culture.

the company inspired an iconic Big Joe Williams blues song, the "King Biscuit Stomp."

In New Orleans and other port cities, vendors made up songs to advertise their wares, giving birth to such songs as "Pepper Pot," "Horseradish Seller" and "Cantaloupe Vendor." Little Milton made a hit in 1969 of a song called "Grits Ain't Groceries." Doc Watson and Clarence Ashley made more than a little innuendo with "Keep My Skillet Good and Greasy."

But far and above the food-inspired tunes that are threaded throughout the African American cultural canon, food and music served a dual purpose of nurturing hope and connection from slavery to the struggles of the civil rights movement. The great African American leader Dorothy Height often said, "If the time is not ripe, we must ripen the times." In the long march to freedom and equality, African American cooks and musicians have creatively conspired to serve something bigger and better than their circumstances might have dictated.

From my early days working in my grandfather's garden to the Bach cantatas we sang at church before a glorious Sunday supper to the rhythm and blues my parents played as they cooked, music was all around me. They say talking to plants helps them grow; I'd like to suggest that cooking without a song—in your heart, if nothing else—is like cooking without salt and pepper. Why would you? And what would you expect the result to be?

I spent decades in Europe as a classically trained opera singer, so you have that influence here too: just the same way that African American cooks in the eighteenth and nineteenth centuries were sometimes sent to Europe to master those techniques and bring them back to our young nation.

This book is a curated set of recipes, a playlist, if you will, of essential African American dishes: the very best of what I have eaten, cooked, and imagined.

Throughout the book, you'll see references to Gullah or Geechee culture. In the Sea Islands off South Carolina and Georgia, African Americans have maintained, for centuries now, a unique culture where the ties to West Africa are more pronounced than almost anywhere else in the continental United States. Julie Dash's film *Daughters of the Dust* remains one of the most powerful depictions of that part of our culture. You might want to screen it with my Gullah Dirty Rice (see page 38).

I was just a little kid when James Beard became the "Dean of American Cuisine," as Julia Child called him. America, pre–James Beard, had a tendency to look upon what was imported as valued, as better.

Beard glorified, elevated, celebrated American culinary expression. He was one of those iconic people who said, "We're cooking American and its fine cooking, and it's worthy of the world's attention."

It has been my life's work to explore and exalt the food of the African diaspora—and the unsung culinary heroes whose innovative farming techniques laid the agrarian economic foundation for America as we know it today. My ancestors combined a gift for technique with a worldly, off-the-charts flavor profile to create a cuisine that could be served with pride from the White House to your mama's house, from ballrooms to juke joints, and everywhere in between.

This book is a curated set of recipes, a playlist, if you will, of essential African American dishes: the very best of what I have eaten, cooked, and imagined. I've divided the book into seven styles of African American music that set the bass line for this medley of meals. Jazz is for starters, the scrumptious riffs that set the

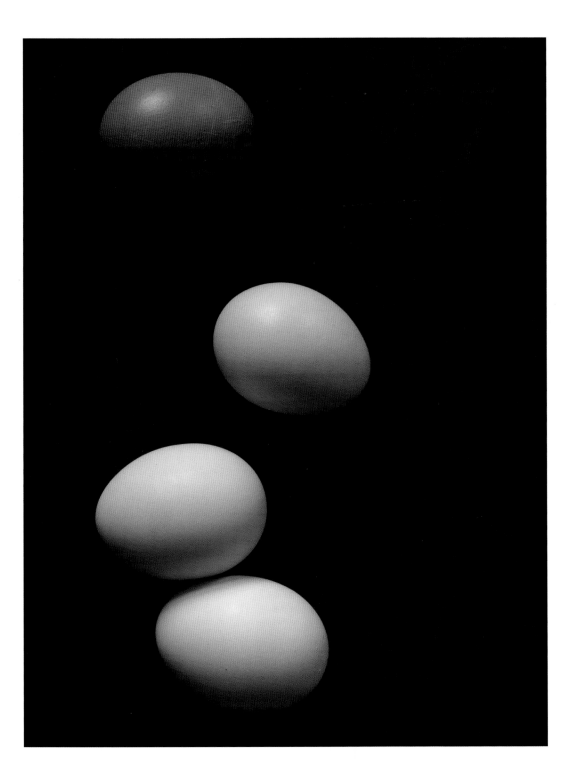

These dishes are easy to master, but so simply elegant that when you serve them, they bring to mind the great Puccini line: "I have lived for art. I have lived for love."

prelude for the meal—although you might find, as I often do, that two or three of these starters make the perfect late-night meal or light weekend lunch.

The section on spirituals is where I've put my rice dishes, my recipes for pasta, grits, and gravies. Spirituals are simple, soulful songs that African American slaves composed to help them survive their darkest days. These dishes make great sides for big meals and are easy one-bowl comfort dishes when your spirits need lifting.

Chapter 3 is all about gospel, gardens, and greens. Gospel music is all about finding the good and praising it. These recipes are joyful vegetable-forward

dishes that taste good, and make you feel good.

My first career was as an opera singer, so the next chapter weaves arias with dishes netted from the sea. These are some of my most beloved dishes, the ones that keep my guests coming back for more: fried catfish, seared grouper with a gumbo sauce, sherry she-crab soup. These dishes are easy to master, but so simply elegant that when you serve them, they bring to mind the great Puccini line: "I have lived for art. I have lived for love."

I have always loved the great divas of African American music, from Leontyne Price and Kathleen Battle to Diana Ross and Tina Turner. I've gathered my big-platter, show-off meat and chicken dishes in honor of these larger-than-life ladies of song. From Roast Quail in Bourbon Cream Sauce (page 121) to Prime Rib Roast with Crawfish Onion Gravy (page 149) to my "so good, you'll wonder how you ever lived without it" Southern Fried Chicken Plate (page 131), these dishes are fun to prepare and even more fun to serve to the ones you love. (But they're too good to share with folks you like just a little bit. You'll have to consult another cookbook for that!)

I grew up in the era of jukeboxes, and to me, that's what a well-stocked pantry is. You don't need much more than butter, flour, milk, and eggs to make my Sweet Potato Muffins (page 170) or my Sage Sausage Biscuits (page 166). And once you've made them, I think you'll find that while they will add the "wow" factor to any meal, they are just as delicious on their own.

I'd be no kind of host if I didn't send you out the door with a song. So I've ended this book with a few sweet serenades. Here you'll find classics like Icebox Lemon Pie (page 183) and Blackberry Cobbler (page 194) as well as my own remixes of old favorites such as my Southern Comfort Peach Shortcake (page 200), Chocolate Pineapple Upside-Down Cake (page 202), and Bourbon Chocolate Praline Truffles (page 206).

I am proud that this book is both a look back and a leap forward. African American cuisine is as evolving as the people from which it came. Alice Waters, of California's Chez Panisse, has said that the great African American chef Edna Lewis helped her look more closely at the bounty of our American culinary heritage. She said that Lewis "showed the deep roots of gastronomy in the United States and that they were really in the South, where we grew for flavor and cooked with sophistication. I had never really considered Southern food before, but I learned from her that it's completely connected to nature, totally in time and place." It's my hope that the recipes in this book will naturally make their way into the rotation of your favorite dishes: connecting you to our shared American heritage, our shared time and place.

1.
Jazz
Starters

Experience is something that just cannot be faked. Jazz alto saxophonist Charlie Parker used to say, "If you don't live it, it won't come out of your horn." And it surely won't come out of your pots.
—*Wynton Marsalis*

Jazz has much in common with cooking, especially when a musician or a cook is trying to find their voice. Jazz is made up of three elements: blues, improvisation, and swing. Those are three components that any home cook knows well.

Blues are the errors you make when you are first learning a dish: undersalting the water (or oversalting—it happens). Not preheating the pan, so your catfish turns out soggy. Or crowding the pan, so the chicken steams instead of frying up with that perfect crispy skin. Even experienced cooks make rookie mistakes. You get distracted or you rush. Leah Chase, the doyenne of New Orleans cooking, once said, "I tell people all the time, you have to be in love with that pot. You have to put all your love in that pot. If you're in a hurry, just eat your sandwich and go. Don't even start cooking, because you can't do anything well in a hurry."

Improvisation is a thread that has always been tightly woven into the history of African American cuisine. The foundations of these recipes were created by men and women who took what they had (which might not have been much), layered it with their favorite flavors, then cooked each dish with as much love and finesse as they could summon.

Swing, I learned from Wynton Marsalis, is that elusive third element that ties an unforgettable jazz song—or an unbelievably delicious meal—together. It's that little extra something that takes it over the top. I can teach you how to cook any one of these recipes. But I can't teach you how to swing—you have to figure that out for yourself.

Your swing might come from the relationship you develop with the butcher at your favorite grocery store, who'll point you to the perfect cut of meat. Or it could be the farmers' market vendor who will put aside her last bunch of candy cane beets just for you.

Improvisation slides right into swing when you start remixing these recipes and making them your own. You might try swapping sriracha for Tabasco in some of these recipes, or pouring my redeye gravy over a plate of stir-fried seitan and crispy green beans.

Sometimes swing asserts itself in the presentation. It may be as simple as the impulse to serve the Lady Lima Succotash Salad with Fresh Mint (page 87) on your grandmother's pink Depression glass plate while Billie Holiday sings "Lady Sings the Blues." Or the wise decision to serve your friends fried chicken on your best wedding china. Swing is that unnameable thing, the thing that makes you smile, that your friends and family may not be able to name but will most *certainly* feel.

In my own home, when I'm serving formally, I like to place platters and trays of interesting starters around the room in the living spaces, usually near the flower arrangements. Being Southern, I love flavorful textured dips eaten with biscuits, crackers, breads, fresh vegetables, or fruit. Perhaps a tray of assorted Deviled Eggs (page 12), Buttermilk Mac and Cheese (page 43), or toasted corn bread canapé with Mustard-Barbecued Chicken Livers (page 25) atop. I'm a fan of easy self-service items guests can help themselves to, creating a more relaxed, informal ambiance. Near the bar I put mixed

Improvisation slides right into swing when you start remixing these recipes and making them your own.

nuts, olives, and crudités, cheese sticks and benne seed crackers, light fare that complements the ritual of bartending. All you need to complete these dishes are a martini, a twist, and a smile.

I wanted to start this book with jazz because it sets the tone for how I hope you'll use it. Find the recipes that call to you right away, look for the sweet spot of harmony: the mix between what the recipe calls for and what feels right for you in your own home kitchen. Then—and this is what makes it like jazz—improvise. Play with it all: ingredients and cooking times, textures and presentations.

Deviled Eggs

Deviled eggs are an iconic American offering, as elegant as they are an ordinary treat. As a Southern boy, it is one of my first memories of eatable love. Few things equal the wallop of flavor you get from a hard-boiled egg white filled with whipped mayonnaise, egg yolks, and bread-and-butter pickle relish, topped with a majestic crown of smoked paprika and cracked black pepper.

When I was growing up in South Carolina, deviled eggs could be found on silver-plated trays at fancy dinner parties as well as church picnic baskets, Sunday dinner tables, and hot Fourth of July barbecues alongside pickled watermelon rind, a candied baked ham, or Ms. Ruthie Mae's crispy fried chicken.

If you want to keep it simple, this recipe is a no-fail favorite. But if you want to take this to the next level, read on for my deviled crab and peppered ham variations.

Makes 24

(continued)

Hard-Boiled Eggs

12 large eggs

1 tablespoon salt

Deviled Eggs

⅓ cup mayonnaise

1 teaspoon dry yellow mustard

¼ cup sweet pickle relish

Salt and pepper

Smoked Spanish paprika, for garnish

Chives, for garnish

For the hard-boiled eggs: Arrange the eggs in a single layer in a large saucepan. Add the salt and enough water to generously cover the eggs. Bring to a boil over high heat, then reduce the heat to low and simmer for 6 minutes. Remove from the heat and let sit for 4 minutes. Drain well. Set aside until cool enough to handle.

For the deviled eggs: Crack the cooled hard-boiled eggs and peel them under cool running water. Carefully dry with paper towels. Slice the eggs in half lengthwise, then transfer the yolks to a bowl and set aside the whites.

Using a fork, mash the yolks until fine. Mix in the mayonnaise, mustard, and relish. Season with salt and pepper. (The filling and the egg whites can be covered and chilled overnight.)

Using a spoon, fill the whites with the yolk mixture. Sprinkle with smoked paprika and chives to garnish. Serve immediately or store in an airtight container overnight to serve the next day.

Variations

Peppered Ham: Sauté ½ cup finely chopped smoked ham in a little oil with cracked black pepper, then fold it into the yolk mixture.

Deviled Crab: Mix ½ cup lump crabmeat with a pinch of cayenne pepper, then fold it into the yolk mixture.

Carolina Bourbon Barbecue Shrimp and Okra Skewers

This dish is akin to West African *suya* or an Asian satay. The Carolina Bourbon Barbecue Sauce is the secret to this recipe's amazing flavor. Bourbon is the South in a bottle, the hard rock of our comfort spirits. It's the way we put the punch in our flavor.

This sauce takes about an hour to make from scratch. It *can* last for six months in the fridge, but it never does. It's just too delicious on everything—from cold fried chicken to your finest roast.

Makes 6 servings

6 (8-inch) wooden skewers, soaked in cold water for 30 minutes

12 medium okra, halved lengthwise

18 extra-large shrimp (preferably tiger shrimp), peeled, tails left intact, and deveined

Vegetable oil, for brushing

Salt and pepper

2 cups Carolina Bourbon Barbecue Sauce (recipe follows)

Heat a gas or charcoal grill to high.

Thread the skewers alternately with the okra and shrimp.

Brush the grill rack with oil. Brush the skewers with oil and season with salt and pepper. Grill the skewers, turning once, until the shrimp are cooked through, about 3 minutes per side.

Remove the skewers from the grill and brush both sides with a generous amount of barbecue sauce. Return the skewers to the grill and cook for 30 seconds on each side.

Serve hot, with additional barbecue sauce on the side.

Carolina Bourbon Barbecue Sauce

This can be served with chicken or fish or any other kind of barbecue, too.

Makes about 4 cups

1 tablespoon olive oil

2 garlic cloves, minced

¼ cup finely chopped onion

2 tablespoons finely chopped celery

2 tablespoons finely chopped red bell pepper

½ cup firmly packed dark brown sugar

2 tablespoons yellow mustard

1½ teaspoons chili powder

1¼ cups ketchup

1 tablespoon Worcestershire sauce

1 tablespoon Tabasco sauce

½ teaspoon cayenne pepper

1 tablespoon red wine vinegar

Salt and pepper

2 tablespoons bourbon

In a large saucepan, heat the oil over medium heat. Add the garlic, onion, celery, and bell pepper and cook, stirring occasionally, until the onion is translucent, about 3 minutes.

Add the brown sugar, mustard, chili powder, ketchup, Worcestershire, Tabasco, cayenne, and vinegar. Season with salt and black pepper. Stir well, bring to a simmer, and reduce the heat to low. Simmer, stirring occasionally, until very thick, about 1 hour.

Remove from the heat and stir in the bourbon. Use immediately or store in sealed containers in the refrigerator for up to 6 months.

Deviled Crab Cakes
with Spicy Creole Mayonnaise

Crab cakes have been a part of Southern seaside cooking for generations. I grew up eating a variety of this amazing delicacy. Crab cakes easily go from gourmet sandwich to perfect appetizer to delicious entrée. They are such an essential part of Southern coastal cooking, and I have had one on every menu of my five restaurants, as well as a featured item on my catering menus for the thirty years I have worked as a chef and restaurateur. In search of more intense flavor over the years, I created what I call Creole mayo when I opened my first restaurant, Café Beulah. I was looking for a more robust yet light sauce to lift the flavor profile. Creole mayo was that sauce, and I've included it here.

These crab cakes and the ones that follow can be made larger and served as an entrée or plated appetizer. As written, they'll be small two-bite passed appetizers.

Makes 6 servings

(continued)

**Deviled Crab Cakes with
Spicy Creole Mayonnaise** (*continued*)

1 pound lump crabmeat, picked over for shells

2 tablespoons finely chopped onion

2 tablespoons finely chopped red bell pepper

2 tablespoons finely chopped celery

1 tablespoon chopped fresh parsley

2 large eggs, beaten

1 cup small cubes white bread, toasted

½ cup plain bread crumbs, plus more for dredging

2 teaspoons finely chopped fresh thyme

1½ teaspoons cayenne pepper

1 cup fresh corn kernels

Salt and pepper

Peanut, canola, or vegetable oil, for frying

Spicy Creole Mayonnaise (recipe follows)

In a large bowl, mix the crab, onion, bell pepper, celery, parsley, eggs, bread cubes, bread crumbs, thyme, cayenne, corn, and ½ teaspoon each salt and black pepper until well combined. Cover and chill for at least 2 hours or up to overnight.

Put more bread crumbs in a shallow bowl. Form the crab mixture into 1-ounce (1½-inch-diameter) patties. Dredge the patties in the bread crumbs to coat and shake off any excess crumbs.

Fill a large cast-iron skillet with oil to a depth of ½ inch. Heat over medium-high heat to 325°F. Working in batches to avoid crowding the skillet, add the crab patties to the hot oil and fry, turning once, until golden brown, about 2 minutes per side.

Drain on a crumpled brown paper bag or paper towels. Serve immediately, with the Spicy Creole Mayonnaise.

Variation

Place the dredged patties on a parchment paper–lined half-sheet pan and coat with nonstick cooking spray. Bake in a preheated 400°F oven until browned, about 5 minutes.

Spicy Creole Mayonnaise

Makes about 3⅓ cups

1 cup canned diced tomatoes

½ cup finely chopped red bell pepper

½ cup finely chopped celery

½ cup finely chopped onion

1 tablespoon light brown sugar

1 teaspoon cayenne pepper

2 tablespoons tomato paste

3 tablespoons red wine vinegar

1 teaspoon salt

½ teaspoon pepper

½ cup mayonnaise

In a medium saucepan, combine the tomatoes, bell pepper, celery, onion, brown sugar, cayenne, tomato paste, vinegar, salt, and black pepper and bring to a boil over medium-high heat, stirring often. Reduce the heat to medium-low and simmer, stirring occasionally, until the mixture has the consistency of a thick paste, about 20 minutes. Let cool to room temperature, then chill for 1 hour.

Transfer the tomato mixture to a food processor and pulse until smooth. Spoon the mixture into a bowl and fold in the mayonnaise. Chill for at least 30 minutes before serving, or store in a sealed container in the refrigerator for up to 1 month.

Hoppin' John Cakes
with Sweet Pepper Rémoulade

Hoppin' John Cakes are, as far as I know, my own very personal invention, the result of years of eating these favorable peas from West Africa and my family being from the Low Country, where people eat rice three times a day.

As a young boy in my mother's kitchen, I started to experiment with leftover peas and rice. I discovered that I could make a patty by combining the rice and peas and adding chopped celery, onions, and spices; the mixture's starch content allowed it to hold its shape while it was frying in my mother's cast-iron skillet. Once I left home I discovered different types of rice have varying starch content so I later added an egg to ensure the patty held up. Eventually, being a kid who loved fried foods, I realized I could take the same mixture, add an egg to bind it, and shape it into a ball I could deep-fry like a hushpuppy. To my family's delight, I made both hoppin' John balls and hushpuppies.

Fast-forward to the opening of my first restaurant, Café Beulah. Looking for signature dishes, I created the Hoppin' John Cake, which was one of my bestselling appetizers at the restaurant and in my catering business. While hoppin' John itself is a very famous Southern dish eaten year-round as a side or with added protein, it easily transforms into a main course.

At New Year's in the South, black-eyed peas and collard greens are served to symbolize good fortune and prosperity. The black-eyed peas represent coins, and the collards dollar bills. With this recipe, your guests will always find themselves in the fortunate column of any meal.

Makes 6 servings

2 tablespoons olive, canola, or vegetable oil,
    plus more for frying
1 tablespoon finely chopped onion
3 garlic cloves, minced
1 tablespoon finely chopped celery
1 tablespoon finely chopped red bell pepper
1/8 teaspoon celery seeds
1/2 teaspoon dried or finely chopped fresh thyme
1/2 teaspoon dried or finely chopped fresh rosemary
1 cup cooked black-eyed peas
1 cup cooked Carolina long-grain rice
1 large egg, beaten
1/8 teaspoon ground nutmeg
3 tablespoons sour cream
1/2 teaspoon cayenne pepper
Salt and pepper
1½ cups plain bread crumbs, plus more for dredging
Sweet Pepper Rémoulade (recipe follows)

In a small skillet, heat the oil over medium heat. Add the onion, garlic, celery, and bell pepper and stir to mix. Add the celery seeds, thyme, and rosemary, mix well, and cook until the onion is translucent, 4 to 5 minutes.

Transfer the mixture to a large bowl and add the black-eyed peas, rice, egg, nutmeg, sour cream, cayenne, and ¼ teaspoon each salt and black pepper. Toss until well mixed.

Transfer half the mixture to a food processor and pulse into a rough paste. Return the mixture to the bowl and mix well, then mix in the bread crumbs. Refrigerate for at least 1 to 2 hours, until stiff.

Put more bread crumbs in a shallow bowl. Form the pea mixture into 1-ounce (1½-inch-diameter) patties. Dredge the patties in the bread crumbs to coat and shake off any excess crumbs.

Fill a large cast-iron skillet with oil to a depth of ½ inch. Heat over medium-high heat to 325°F. Working in batches to avoid crowding the skillet, add the patties to the hot oil and fry, turning once, until golden brown, about 2 minutes per side.

Drain on a crumpled brown paper bag or paper towels. Serve immediately, with the rémoulade.

Sweet Pepper Rémoulade

Makes about 1¼ cups

¾ cup mayonnaise

2 tablespoons Dijon mustard

1 tablespoon whole-grain Dijon mustard

1 teaspoon Tabasco sauce

2 garlic cloves, minced

¼ cup diced roasted peppers

Salt and pepper

In a food processor, combine the mayonnaise, both mustards, Tabasco, garlic, and roasted peppers and puree until smooth. Taste and season with salt and black pepper. Chill in a sealed container for at least 1 hour or until ready to serve, up to 1 month.

Mustard-Barbecued Chicken Livers on Peppered Turnip Greens

For this dish, I took two dishes that were my favorite as a child and combined them. Turnip greens have always been my favorite green. As a child in my grandfather's city garden, I would help tend to those greens like a jealous lover waiting excitedly for harvest. I get the same feeling of joyful expectation every time I make this dish.

Fried chicken livers are the Southern equivalent of foie gras, a delicacy equally desirable as a takeout item or on the finest table. Mustard barbecue sauce was born in South Carolina and is a one-of-a-kind sauce. It is perfectly suited for the crispy livers, but really embraces the strong flavor of the turnip greens. With the added cracked black pepper (you can add bird's-eye chile for even more heat), this is an unforgettable Southern dish.

Makes 6 servings

5 tablespoons olive oil

1 bunch green onions, finely chopped

2 teaspoons minced garlic

½ cup unsalted chicken or vegetable stock

3 large bunches turnip greens, tough stems discarded and leaves coarsely chopped

½ cup all-purpose flour, for dredging

1 pint chicken livers, washed until the water runs clear and patted dry

Salt and pepper

1 teaspoon cracked black pepper

½ cup Mustard Barbecue Sauce (recipe follows), warmed

In a large saucepot, heat 2 tablespoons of the oil over medium-high heat. Add the green onions and garlic and cook, stirring, until the garlic is golden, 1 to 2 minutes. Reduce the heat to medium, add the stock, and bring to a boil. Add the greens by the fistful, stirring to coat the greens with the stock and adding more greens as they shrink. Reduce the heat to medium-low. Cover and simmer until the greens are very tender, 30 to 45 minutes.

(continued)

Mustard-Barbecued Chicken Livers
on Peppered Turnip Greens (*continued*)

In a large skillet, heat the remaining 3 tablespoons oil over medium-high heat until hot but not smoking. Line a plate with paper towels and set it nearby.

Put the flour in a shallow bowl. Season the livers with 1 teaspoon each salt and black pepper. Lightly dredge them in the flour, shaking off any excess. Working in batches to avoid crowding the skillet, add the livers to the hot oil and fry, turning once, until golden and crisp, about 1½ minutes per side. Do not let them overcook. Drain on paper towels.

Stir the cracked pepper into the greens. Taste and season with salt. Transfer to a platter and top with the livers. Drizzle with the Mustard Barbecue Sauce and serve immediately.

Mustard Barbecue Sauce

Makes 4 cups

3 tablespoons olive oil

4 garlic cloves, minced

½ cup finely chopped onion

1 celery stalk, finely chopped

¼ cup finely chopped red bell pepper

1½ cups yellow mustard

1 cup firmly packed light brown sugar

1 tablespoon chili powder

3 tablespoons red wine vinegar

1 tablespoon Worcestershire sauce

¼ cup Tabasco sauce

1 teaspoon cayenne pepper

1 teaspoon ground nutmeg

Salt and pepper

In a medium stockpot, heat the oil over medium-high heat. Add the garlic, onion, celery, and bell pepper and cook, stirring occasionally, until the onion is translucent, about 5 minutes. Add the mustard, brown sugar, chili powder, vinegar, Worcestershire, Tabasco, cayenne, nutmeg, and a pinch each of salt and black pepper. Stir well and bring to a light boil.

Reduce the heat to low and simmer for 1 hour. Let cool to room temperature, then use immediately or store in an airtight container in the refrigerator for up to 6 months.

Do the best you
can until you
know better.
Then when you
know better,
do better.
—*Maya Angelou*

2.
Spirituals

Rice,
Pasta,
and Grits:
Comfort
Things

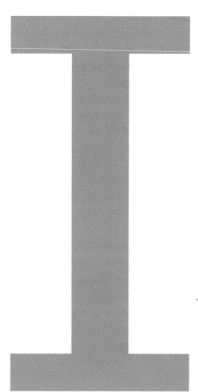I've always believed there was a direct line between the comfort of spirituals and the solace we take in our comfort foods. These are simple "Lean on Me" dishes that become the backbone of a home cook's repertoire.

In the days of slavery, African Americans weren't allowed to gather for church services, as slave owners feared that any formal gathering might set the stage for revolt and rebellion. But the inhumane, brutal conditions meant that faith, and prayer, were essential tools of survival for slaves. Spirituals took Christian Bible stories and married them to melodies that lifted the spirit and lyrics that encouraged hope even during the darkest days. Some spirituals, such as "Swing Low, Sweet Chariot," were so popular that they outgrew their genre and became cornerstones of the American folk tradition.

As a kid, I spent my summers working in my grandpa's city garden. He worked an acre of vegetables in his backyard, which became a source of education and nurturing for my family and me. I used to love tending the vegetables: picking the beans, tomatoes, and okra. Digging up the potatoes, I would while the hours away singing spirituals or Baptist hymns like "Deep River," "Great Day the Righteous Kingdom," "Swing Low, Sweet Chariot," and my favorite, "Let Us Break Bread Together." I would lose myself in the field, caught up in my song and playing in the dirt, living in every verse I could remember. Music, as it so often does, helped make those chores a joy rather than work.

My grandfather worked in the rice fields of the Low Country as a teenager. At one point, South Carolina furnished the majority of rice for the thirteen original American colonies. Rice was king in South Carolina, and the wealth of the state came from rice farming. In this section, you'll find recipes for some of my favorite rice dishes, including Carolina Hoppin' John (Rice and Peas) (page 34), Charleston Spicy Red Rice (page 36), and Gullah Dirty Rice (page 38). Besides my beloved rice, in this chapter I pay homage to three African American essentials: mac and cheese, grits, and gravy.

Mac and cheese smacks of Southern eating much like a pot of collard greens, pot likker, and corn bread do. The stories about how this "wannabe Italian" dish became Southern are many, and the truth is anybody's guess. Wading through the many tales of its origins in America, the one that seems most credible is that it came via missionaries: churchgoers from England who settled in Connecticut. Some say Thomas Jefferson brought the idea back from Europe and had his cook or house attendant re-create the dish, and it subsequently took off in the South. None of this is important to the many Southern African American homes, soul food restaurants, church dinners, and picnics around the South that feature the dish.

In the late 1930s, Kraft put macaroni in a box, and the rest is history. Every Southern culinary and kitchen queen perfected her version of this recipe. It

Spirituals took Christian Bible stories and married them to melodies that lifted the spirit and lyrics that encouraged hope even during the darkest days.

was always a special Sunday meal when I saw my mother's Pyrex casserole on the table alongside a platter of fried chicken and buttered biscuits, not unlike the casseroles and plated dishes I would later enjoy while living in Europe, particularly in Italy: pasta dishes with fontina, provolone, Parmesan, and a great cheese sauce. My mac and cheese recipes start on page 43.

Grits (also known as stone-ground hominy) are as much a Southern staple as our beloved rice. As versatile and agreeable as rice but creamy, we like to call grits "a party in a bowl." Like rice, grits take on the flavor of whatever they're

Grits are a destination for Southerners. It's how we greet the day, how we say "welcome" to a friend or a stranger.

served with. What they offer a dish is a foundation of texture, a willing sponge to hold flavor. They're truly satisfying in every way.

A bowl of grits and gravy goes with everything. I proudly serve it all the time. It also makes a terrific meal for one. When I'm dining solo, I top it with a fried egg or savory sausage bits, and I indulge when alone, sometimes topping it carbonara-style with bits of bacon, sweet peas, and a little chile oil. In this chapter, you'll find both my basic Stone-Ground Grits (page 51) and my Grits and Sage Sausage Gravy (page 52).

Grits are a destination for Southerners. It's how we greet the day, how we say "welcome" to a friend or a stranger.

Gravy is the ambassador of flavor for the taste buds. It is also the saving grace for every dish teetering on the brink of greatness and disaster. It is the sauce that stretched the meal—if not *made* the meal—when all a family could afford was a little bit of meat. Serve a boat of gravy with a pan of biscuits or crackling corn bread, and the gravy made sure everybody ate—and ate well.

Gravy can take your dish from ordinary to extraordinary. Done right, it's the magic in your pot, giving you that extra opportunity to say something unique and special about how you interpret a treasured recipe. The word *gravy*, even in our everyday vernacular, speaks to something extra, prosperity, and indulgence. It's an embellishment, that additional lyrical moment you create in a song that truly moves you. Everyone who has ever seen a singer perform live is familiar with the extra notes we call riffs. Just as those vocal gymnastics help a singer own a rendition of a song, gravy brings that added something to your perfect dish. It's a humble ingredient that denotes and conveys your richest and most decadent expression. You may just want to skip ahead to page 53, where you'll find my Smothered Shrimp and Crabmeat Pan Gravy.

Carolina Hoppin' John (Rice and Peas)

As basic as red beans and rice are in Latin America, black-eyed peas and rice are beloved in the Carolinas.

Makes 6 servings

2 tablespoons olive oil

2 cups Carolina long-grain rice

1 small onion, finely diced

1 garlic clove, minced

½ cup finely diced red bell pepper

1 large jalapeño, finely diced

1 cup frozen black-eyed peas, thawed

¼ cup finely diced celery

2 bay leaves

2 teaspoons Creole seasoning

2 tablespoons minced fresh parsley

2 tablespoons unsalted butter

4 cups unsalted chicken or vegetable stock

Salt and pepper

¾ cup sliced green onions

In a large saucepan, heat the oil over medium heat. Add the rice, onion, and garlic. Cook, stirring often, until the rice is toasted and the onion is translucent, about 5 minutes.

Add the bell pepper, jalapeño, black-eyed peas, celery, bay leaves, Creole seasoning, parsley, butter, and stock. Season with salt and black pepper. Stir well, cover, and bring to a boil over medium-high heat. Reduce the heat to low and cook, covered, until the rice is tender, about 20 minutes.

Discard the bay leaves. Fold in the green onions and serve.

Charleston Spicy Red Rice

Thirty years ago, in the days before Uber and Lyft, the *Washington Post* sent a reporter to cover the Symposium on American Cuisine in Charleston, South Carolina. Discouraged by the tablecloth restaurants' offering of "balsamic vinegar and phyllo" instead of butter beans and corn bread, the *Post* published a recipe for red rice from a Carolina cabdriver known simply as "R.A.Y." What made his recipe such a hoot was the suggestion for the side dishes. He recommended that you serve the rice with "barbecued pork, fried fish, fish cakes, chicken, pork chops or more sausage." To me, that was all the fact-checking you needed to know that "R.A.Y." was real. This dish is centerpiece-worthy, but in Carolina, we like it on a table surrounded by meat, pork, and, if you've got it, some delicious fried fish.

Charleston Spicy Red Rice comes to us by way of West Africa, where it is known as jollof rice. African slaves brought this traditional dish to the new world and made it a staple in the Gullah communities of the Sea Islands. A simple but elegant dish, it is very inexpensive and can be a complete meal for a family when served with beans or your favorite vegetables. Dad, ever the Geechee, would always add shrimp, crab, or fish. He loved grouper or porgies. Preparing spicy red rice, you felt like you were honoring the ancestors, carrying on customs and traditions that connected you to the continent of Africa. For African Americans who had been stolen from their families, traditions, and culture, this dish summoned an amazing feeling of being nurtured and carried back home.

Makes 6 servings

2 tablespoons olive oil

2 cups Carolina long-grain rice

1 small onion, finely diced

1 garlic clove, minced

¼ cup finely diced celery

¼ cup finely diced red bell pepper

1 cup tomato puree

1 tablespoon tomato paste

1 teaspoon cayenne pepper

1 bay leaf

2 tablespoons minced fresh parsley

2 tablespoons unsalted butter

3½ cups unsalted chicken or vegetable stock

Salt and pepper

In a large saucepan, heat the oil over medium heat. Add the rice, onion, and garlic. Cook, stirring often, until the rice is toasted and the onion is translucent, about 5 minutes.

Add the celery, bell pepper, tomato puree, tomato paste, cayenne, bay leaf, parsley, butter, and stock. Season with salt and black pepper. Stir well, cover, and bring to a boil over medium-high heat. Reduce the heat to low and cook, covered, until the rice is tender, about 20 minutes.

Fluff with a fork. Discard the bay leaf and serve.

This dish is centerpiece-worthy, but in Carolina, we like it on a table surrounded by meat, pork, and, if you've got it, some delicious fried fish.

Gullah Dirty Rice

This is a relatively simple dish inspired by red river rice or Louisiana's jambalaya. Not unlike dirty rice from the Cajun culture, Gullah rice is a catchall rice, a way to create a one-dish meal full of flavor.

Makes 6 servings

5 cups unsalted chicken or vegetable stock

½ cup chicken gizzards

3 tablespoons unsalted butter

1 cup chicken livers, washed until the water runs clear and patted dry

Salt and pepper

2 tablespoons olive oil

2 cups Carolina long-grain rice

1 small onion, finely chopped

1 garlic clove, minced

1 teaspoon sweet paprika

½ teaspoon cayenne pepper

½ cup chopped green onions

2 teaspoons Tabasco sauce

2 tablespoons minced fresh parsley

In a medium saucepan, bring 1 cup of the stock to a simmer over medium heat. Add the gizzards. Reduce the heat to medium-low, cover, and simmer until tender, about 30 minutes. Drain the gizzards, then chop them.

Meanwhile, in a large skillet, melt 1 tablespoon of the butter over medium-high heat. Sprinkle the livers with salt and black pepper and add them to the skillet. Cook, turning occasionally, until lightly browned outside and still pink in the centers, about 5 minutes. Transfer to a cutting board and let rest for 20 minutes. Chop the livers.

In a large saucepan, heat the oil over medium heat. Add the rice, onion, and garlic. Cook, stirring often, until the rice is toasted and the onion is translucent, about 5 minutes. Add the paprika, cayenne, green onions, Tabasco, parsley, gizzards, liver, the remaining 4 cups stock, and the remaining 2 tablespoons butter. Season with salt and black pepper.

Stir well, cover, and bring to a boil over medium-high heat. Reduce the heat to low and cook, covered, until the rice is tender, about 20 minutes.

Taste and season with salt and black pepper. Fluff with a fork and serve.

Savory Chicken Bog

The key to upping the comfort level of this dish is making extra gravy. There are very few people who can deny the inherent comfort of a rich chicken-and-gravy dish like this. Where I grew up, everybody's mama, aunt or uncle, cousin, caretaker, or church lady who cooked made a version of this dish. You could eat seven versions, seven days in a row, and proclaim them all to be the best meal you ever had. This is one of those simple dishes that, once you've mastered, becomes imbued with something much greater than the food on the plate. It's a memory, an emotional swell that will be triggered every time you make the dish.

The chicken bog should have a similar texture to a risotto with lots of meat and vegetables. If the mixture is too loose or watery, cook, uncovered, stirring often, over medium-low heat until the liquid cooks off and the dish reaches a wet-rice consistency.

Makes 6 servings

(continued)

Savory Chicken Bog (*continued*)

1 (2- to 3-pound) whole chicken, or 6 bone-in,
    skin-on chicken thighs, excess fat trimmed

6 cups unsalted chicken stock

1 cup finely chopped onion

1 teaspoon coarsely ground black pepper

Salt and pepper

3 tablespoons olive oil

2 cups Carolina long-grain rice

1½ teaspoons minced garlic

1 cup finely chopped celery

1 large sprig fresh thyme

2 bay leaves

1 teaspoon rubbed sage

1 teaspoon cayenne pepper

½ pound smoked sausage, sliced

In a large saucepot, combine the chicken, stock, onion, black pepper, and 1 teaspoon salt. Bring to a boil over medium-high heat. Cover, reduce the heat to low, and cook until the chicken is cooked through and tender, about 40 minutes.

Remove the chicken from the pot and set aside until cool enough to handle; reserve the cooking liquid. Discard the skin and bones of the chicken and chop the meat into bite-size pieces. Skim off and discard the fat from the cooking liquid.

In a large saucepan, heat the oil over medium heat. Add the rice and cook, stirring often, until toasted, about 5 minutes. Add the garlic and cook, stirring often, until golden, about 2 minutes. Add the celery, thyme, bay leaves, sage, cayenne, and 4 cups of the reserved cooking liquid. Stir well, cover, and bring to a boil over medium-high heat. Add the chopped chicken and the sausage.

Cover and boil for 20 minutes, then reduce the heat to low. If mixture is too watery, cook, uncovered, stirring often, over medium-low heat until the liquid reaches the desired bog consistency. Serve hot.

Buttermilk Mac and Cheese

For me, Buttermilk Mac and Cheese always conjures up the joy that is a lifetime of Sundays.

Buttermilk Mac and Cheese (*continued*)

As a kid, I loved Sunday school, but the church service afterward was long and tiring. My mother would let me rest my head on her lap, where I never failed to fall promptly to sleep. My dreams were filled with the feast that would be waiting for us back home, which always seemed to include some version of this dish. For me, Buttermilk Mac and Cheese always conjures up the joy that is a lifetime of Sundays.

Makes 6 servings

½ pound cavatelli or other small shell-shaped pasta

3 tablespoons unsalted butter, plus more for the dish

3 tablespoons all-purpose flour

1 cup whole milk

1 cup buttermilk

1 cup heavy cream

1¼ pounds sharp Cheddar cheese, shredded

2 large eggs, beaten

Salt and pepper

In a medium stockpot, bring 8 cups water to a boil. Add the pasta and cook according to the package directions until al dente, about 8 minutes. Drain, rinse with cold water, and drain again.

Meanwhile, preheat the oven to 350°F. Butter a 2-quart casserole dish.

In a large saucepan, melt the butter over medium heat. Add the flour and whisk until thick and creamy, 1 to 2 minutes. While whisking, add the milk, buttermilk, and cream. Cook, whisking continuously, until the mixture reaches a custard consistency, about 5 minutes.

Add two-thirds of the cheese and cook, stirring, until melted. Remove from the heat and slowly stir in the eggs. Add the pasta and stir until well coated. Season with salt and pepper.

Pour half the mixture into the prepared casserole dish. Sprinkle with half the remaining cheese. Pour over the remaining pasta mixture and top with the remaining cheese.

Bake until the top is toasted and crusty, about 30 minutes. Let rest for 5 to 10 minutes before serving.

Variations

Rosemary Spiked: Stir ¼ cup rosemary oil into the pasta mixture.

Wilted Spinach: Mix wilted spinach into the pasta mixture.

Deviled Crab: Season lump crabmeat with Old Bay seasoning and cayenne pepper and mix it into the pasta mixture.

Dunbar Pie: Macaroni with Meat Sauce

In South Carolina, we do a Dunbar pie, which is basically mac and cheese with a ground beef tomato sauce, kind of like a lasagna with beef ragù.

As a caterer, I created a concept for my clients that I called "Macaroni and Cheese Night." This was a theme party that consisted of as many as five or more different types of mac and cheese. The offerings ranged from the traditional pie to versions with spinach, shrimp and crabmeat gravy, lamb ragù, truffle and chanterelle mushrooms, and gumbo with crispy okra. It was always a hit.

Makes 6 servings

1 pound elbow macaroni

2 tablespoons olive oil

1½ pounds ground beef chuck

Salt and pepper

2 teaspoons red pepper flakes

4 garlic cloves, minced

1 cup diced onion

1 tablespoon dried oregano

2 tablespoons tomato paste

½ cup diced red bell pepper

3½ cups canned diced tomatoes

2 cups tomato sauce

1 cup unsalted chicken stock

1 cup heavy cream

½ cup chopped fresh parsley

¼ cup chopped fresh mint

3 cups grated sharp Cheddar cheese

In a medium stockpot, bring 8 cups water to a boil. Add the macaroni and cook according to the package directions until al dente. Drain, rinse with cold water, and drain again.

Meanwhile, preheat the oven to 350°F.

In a large saucepot, heat the oil over medium heat. Add the ground beef and season with salt and black pepper. Cook, stirring and breaking the meat into crumbles as it cooks, until lightly browned and cooked through, about 10 minutes.

Add the red pepper flakes, garlic, onion, and oregano. Cook, stirring often, until the onion is translucent, about 5 minutes. Add the tomato paste, bell pepper, diced tomatoes, tomato sauce, stock, and cream. Season with salt and black pepper. Bring to a light boil over medium-high heat, stirring occasionally.

Reduce the heat to medium and cook, stirring occasionally, until thickened, about 10 minutes. Turn off the heat. Stir in the parsley and mint, then stir in the pasta.

Spoon half the pasta mixture into a 3-quart casserole dish. Sprinkle with half the cheese, then spoon in the remaining pasta. Top with the remaining cheese.

Bake until the sauce is bubbling and the cheese is browned, 35 to 40 minutes. Let rest for 10 minutes before serving.

Macaroni Vegetable Salad

In the summertime, I can never get enough of macaroni salad. This dish reminds me of my aunt Daisy, who was a cook in New York City. Whenever she came back home to South Carolina, I could really look forward to some great eating. Like any great cook, she took all kinds of liberties in bringing this dish to life. Sometimes she added the freshest garden vegetables; other times, it was tuna, chicken, even shrimp. In her hands, a humble pasta salad went from a side dish to the main course in a flash.

Like the Italians, Aunt Daisy would say the secret is to not overcook the pasta. She also believed that things tasted better when you gave them flavor from the beginning, so where my mother would simply boil the macaroni in water, Aunt Daisy would cook it in seasoned water, like chicken stock or the pot likker from savory greens. Experiment with adding herbs or your favorite tasty fat to the liquid when you boil the pasta.

This dish also calls for sweet pickle relish, but smart cooks go the extra distance, chopping bread-and-butter pickles into small cubes and splashing the pasta with a little of the pickle juice to reaffirm that flavor. I also like to cut my hard-boiled eggs slightly larger so their flavor is more pronounced.

While it seems simple enough, the measure and creativity of the chef can really elevate this Southern specialty. This is a treat with Sunday dinners, but don't hesitate to make this for a Monday- or Tuesday-night supper when you need a lift. Served alongside a grocery store rotisserie chicken, this is summer on a plate, even in the dead of winter.

Makes 6 servings

2 cups broccoli florets

1 tablespoon olive oil

Salt and pepper

3 cups cooked macaroni, rinsed and cooled

4 hard-boiled eggs (see page 15), chopped

¼ cup chopped celery

¼ cup chopped onion

½ cup frozen green peas, thawed

1 cup halved grape tomatoes

¼ cup chopped roasted red bell pepper

1 tablespoon sugar

1 tablespoon white wine vinegar

½ cup mayonnaise

1 teaspoon Dijon mustard

¼ cup chopped fresh parsley

Preheat the oven to 450°F.

On a half-sheet pan, toss the broccoli with the oil, season with salt and black pepper, and arrange the florets in a single layer. Roast until tender, about 30 minutes.

In a large bowl, combine the roasted broccoli, macaroni, eggs, celery, onion, peas, tomatoes, bell pepper, sugar, vinegar, mayonnaise, mustard, and parsley. Toss until well combined. Taste and season with salt and black pepper

Cover and chill for at least 1 hour or up to overnight. If chilled overnight, let it sit out for at least 30 minutes before serving.

This is a treat with Sunday dinners, but don't hesitate to make this for a Monday- or Tuesday-night supper when you need a lift.

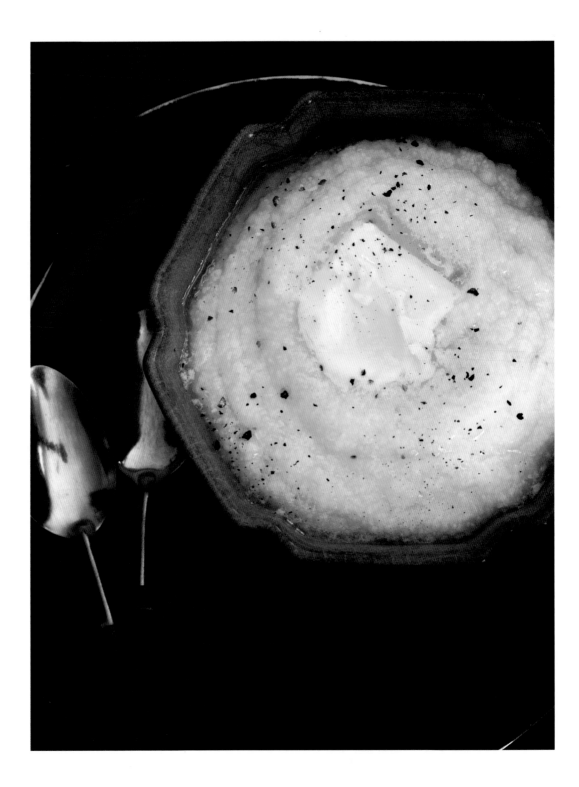

Stone-Ground Grits

Like rice and pasta, grits are best when you give flavor to the dish from the start. Mother would, at my father's request, fry bacon or fatback and add the grease to the boiling water before she cooked grits. As a chef, I cook my grits in protein stock, depending on the toppings, or a seasoned vegetable stock, like pot likker from greens or cabbage. The cooking liquid from boiled root vegetables works nicely as well.

Makes 6 servings

4 cups unsalted vegetable or chicken stock, plus
    more if needed

2 tablespoons unsalted butter, plus more for
    serving if desired

1 tablespoon olive oil

1 teaspoon salt

½ teaspoon pepper

1¾ cups stone-ground white grits

In a heavy-bottomed saucepan, combine the stock, butter, oil, salt, and pepper and bring to boil over high heat. Reduce the heat to medium. While whisking, pour in the grits. Bring to a steady boil and cook for 5 minutes.

Reduce the heat to low, give the grits a good stir, and cover. Simmer until tender, creamy, and thick, about 15 minutes. If the mixture becomes too stiff and dry before the grits are cooked through, add additional stock. When the grits are done, you can add more stock if you prefer a thinner consistency.

Serve immediately, topped with more butter, if desired.

Variation

Grits with Stewed Greens: Spoon Stewed Collard Greens with Smoked Turkey (page 95) over the grits.

Grits and Sage Sausage Gravy

Now, gravy is all about the quality and flavor of your ingredients. My secret is to use pan drippings as part of the stock for a more intense flavor, but don't underestimate the roux. To some Southern cooks, roux is everything, and the darker your roux, the better. Getting the roux just right takes the patience and care of a particular disposition. I have seen the famed actor Danny Glover take a bar stool and sit in front of the stove for an hour or more, stirring his roux with the patience of a saint.

Makes 6 servings

¾ pound fresh sage sausage or breakfast sausage, casings removed, if needed

½ tablespoon unsalted butter

2½ tablespoons all-purpose flour

1 cup unsalted chicken stock

1 cup heavy cream

½ teaspoon Worcestershire sauce

⅛ teaspoon ground nutmeg

Salt and pepper

1 recipe Stone-Ground Grits (page 51), hot

In a heavy-bottomed medium saucepan, cook the sausage over medium heat, breaking it up as it cooks, until browned and cooked through, about 5 minutes. Transfer the sausage to a plate. Drain all but 3 tablespoons of the fat from the pan.

Add the butter to the pan, increase the heat to medium-high, and whisk in the flour. Cook, whisking continuously, until the mixture is dark brown, 3 to 5 minutes. While whisking, drizzle in the stock and cook, whisking, until the sauce thickens, about 5 minutes more.

While whisking, slowly pour in the cream, then whisk in the Worcestershire and nutmeg. Season with salt and pepper and whisk for 2 minutes more. Stir in the sausage. Reduce the heat to medium-low and simmer for 3 minutes.

Spoon the sausage gravy over the hot grits and serve immediately.

Smothered Shrimp and Crabmeat Pan Gravy

If gravy represents the good things in life, it doesn't get much more luxe than this.

Smothered Shrimp and Crabmeat Pan Gravy (continued)

Joni Mitchell once sang, "Some get the gravy, some get the gristle." If gravy represents the good things in life, it doesn't get much more luxe than this. I can hardly imagine a gravy richer than one made with shrimp, crabmeat, and pan drippings.

Makes 10 to 12 servings

3 tablespoons unsalted butter

4 garlic cloves, finely chopped

1 large onion, chopped

2 celery stalks, finely chopped

1 red bell pepper, finely chopped

¼ cup vegetable or olive oil

½ cup all-purpose flour

2 tablespoons rubbed sage

1 tablespoon finely chopped fresh thyme

½ cup dry sherry

¼ cup Worcestershire sauce

¼ teaspoon ground nutmeg

½ teaspoon cayenne pepper

3 cups clam juice, fish stock, or chicken stock

1 tablespoon tomato paste

Salt and pepper

3 pounds peeled and deveined jumbo shrimp, butterflied with tails intact

1½ pounds jumbo lump crabmeat, picked over for shells

2 recipes Stone-Ground Grits (page 51), hot

In a large heavy-bottomed stockpot, melt the butter over medium heat. Add the garlic, onion, celery, and bell pepper. Cook, stirring often, until the onion is translucent, about 10 minutes.

In a separate frying pan, heat the oil over medium heat. Add the flour and stir briskly. Cook, stirring continuously, until the roux begins to brown, being careful not to burn it, 15 to 20 minutes.

Transfer the roux to the pot with the vegetables. Stir in the sage, thyme, sherry, Worcestershire, nutmeg, cayenne, and clam juice. Increase the heat to medium-high and cook, stirring continuously, until the mixture begins to simmer lightly and everything gets agitated. Stir in the tomato paste and season with salt and black pepper. Reduce the heat to medium and cook, stirring often, until creamy and thick, about 15 minutes.

Add the shrimp and cook until just cooked through, 3 to 4 minutes. Reduce the heat to medium-low. Fold in the crabmeat and simmer until heated through, about 2 minutes. Taste and season with salt and pepper.

Plate the grits in a casserole or deep-dish platter, then ladle the shrimp and crabmeat gravy on top. Serve immediately.

3.

Field Greens and Green Things

Gospel

Greens are a
dish that most
Southerners would
walk a mile for.
—*Edna Lewis*

For me, gospel is synonymous with Mahalia Jackson. I loved watching the occasional appearance by Mahalia Jackson on variety TV or *The Ed Sullivan Show*. Mahalia was a diva, a real queen of song and movement, much like the opera divas I admired like Leontyne Price, Marian Anderson, and Maria Callas.

We attended a black Baptist church where once the old Jubilee choir finished exhausting the virtues of a raggedy hymn as only they could, the junior choir would elevate the moment with a Bach cantata or a spirited art song by Brahms or Mozart. It was an unusual medley of culture that found harmony in my hometown Southern church.

Every garden is a form of prayer. As a young boy, the stabilizer in my daily adventures was my grandfather, the larger-than-life, loveable but strong and powerful man whom I called Papa.

My most favorite time was with Papa in his vegetable garden. This was our sacred place. In the garden he tended, Papa seemed open and free. While we worked in the garden, he would tell me stories of his childhood. He would talk about the importance of farming, of knowing the land and where your food came from. He taught me the glory of eating what you farmed and harvested.

Papa was a spiritual man. He was not much of a churchgoer, but what I understood was that his garden was his church, his sanctuary, where he spoke with God. It was an honor to work the land with him and to help in some way harvest the offerings of his garden, his bounty.

I felt the garden was where he visited the ancestors, his parents, who were farmers—and slaves. I always felt like when I left that garden, I had visited with the spirits who rested there, an invisible force that only my grandpa really knew and understood. For me, it was just magical, a world away from this one that I could escape to with a simple swing of the garden door.

There's much to partake of in this harvest of vegetable recipes, but look out especially for my potato salad recipe. I love potato salad, and I am convinced it loves me. My Sweet Pickle Potato Salad will make you the star of every family reunion, company picnic, and potluck. Just go ahead and skip to page 80.

In the garden he tended, Papa seemed open and free. While we worked in the garden, he would tell me stories of his childhood.

Carolina Cabbage Slaw with Roasted Sweet Corn

I have so many memories of sitting at the picnic table in my parents' backyard, shucking corn with family and friends. We'd shuck bushels at a time while sipping large glasses of iced tea. Cool drinks and big belly laughs made the time fly by, as did dishes like this; the promise of roasted sweet corn was always an incentive.

Another way to do this at home is to season the ears of corn and throw them under the broiler on a sheet pan.

Makes 6 servings

4 medium ears corn, shucked

½ cup olive oil

1 large head savoy cabbage, cored and shredded

1 (5-ounce) bag baby spinach

½ cup mayonnaise

¼ cup sweet pickle relish

1 tablespoon Dijon mustard

1 teaspoon celery seeds

¼ teaspoon cayenne pepper

⅛ teaspoon ground nutmeg

Salt and pepper

Heat a grill to medium-high.

Brush the corn with ¼ cup of the oil. Grill the corn, turning occasionally, until tender and charred in spots, about 13 minutes. Set the corn aside until cool enough to handle, then cut the kernels from the cobs.

In a large bowl, combine the roasted corn, the remaining ¼ cup oil, the cabbage, spinach, mayonnaise, relish, mustard, celery seeds, cayenne, and nutmeg. Taste and season with salt and black pepper. Cover and chill for several hours before serving.

Field Greens, Poached Pear, and Black-Eyed Pea Salad
with Citrus Vinaigrette

This salad is, for me, about flavor, texture, and childhood memories.

As a boy, my father came home one day with a baby pear tree and planted it in our backyard. Watching that tree grow was an exciting proposition to a child. I will never forget the first buds, and later the tiny fruits that began to grow. First there were only a few, but each year there were more. Over the years, the tree grew like a large wishbone switch. My father loved that tree and would use its fruit to make everything from pear preserves to canned pears, which he would put in large Mason jars and pass out proudly to friends and family. One year, he and my grandfather made pear brandy. Their version of Calvados, no doubt.

When I opened my first restaurant, I served this salad, a way of honoring my father and his pears. This is a truly versatile salad that can easily go from appetizer to full meal. The beans give it generous protein, and the sweet, savory dressing brings it all together. Not to mention the perfect drunken pear. You could most certainly simply cut up fresh pears, but poaching them adds extra flavor, texture, and elegance.

A late-night tip: I would often make this salad before going out and leave it undressed. Then when I returned home late at night with friends, I'd toss it with the dressing. It's a perfect light-but-filling late-night meal.

Makes 8 servings

(continued)

When I opened my first restaurant, I served this salad, a way of honoring my father and his pears.

**Field Greens, Poached Pear, and Black-Eyed Pea Salad
with Citrus Vinaigrette** (*continued*)

4 ripe but firm Bosc pears, halved and cored

2 cups red wine

1 cup sugar

2 cinnamon sticks

2 star anise pods

1½ cups halved grape tomatoes

1 red onion, halved and thinly sliced

2 cups thinly sliced seedless cucumbers

2 pounds mixed salad greens

2½ cups cooked black-eyed peas

Citrus Vinaigrette (recipe follows)

In a medium saucepan, combine the pears, wine, sugar, cinnamon sticks, star anise, and 1 cup water. Bring to a boil over medium-high heat. Cover, reduce the heat to low, and poach until the pears are tender but not mushy, about 35 minutes. Let the pears cool to room temperature in the poaching liquid, then cover and chill for at least several hours or up to overnight.

Remove the pears from the poaching liquid and cut them lengthwise into ⅛-inch-thick slices. Reserve the poaching liquid for another use.

In a large bowl, toss the grape tomatoes, onion, cucumbers, and greens to combine. Add the black-eyed peas and the vinaigrette and toss.

Divide the salad among eight chilled plates. Garnish with the poached pears and serve immediately.

Citrus Vinaigrette

Makes about 1½ cups

¼ cup Champagne vinegar

1 tablespoon fresh lime juice

1 tablespoon fresh lemon juice

1 tablespoon fresh orange juice

1½ teaspoons minced shallot

½ teaspoon Dijon mustard

2 tablespoons mayonnaise

1½ teaspoons honey

Salt and pepper

¾ cup extra-virgin olive oil

In a food processor, combine the vinegar, citrus juices, shallot, mustard, mayonnaise, honey, and a pinch each of salt and pepper and pulse until smooth, about 30 seconds. With the machine running, add the oil in a thin stream and process until emulsified. Taste and season with salt and pepper. Use immediately or store in an airtight container in the refrigerator for up to 3 days.

Creole Caesar Salad with Corn Bread Croutons

My love for okra began as a child and continues to border on just this side of insanity.

I *love* okra.

As a young boy, I would smuggle a brown bag full of fried okra into the movies as my better-than-popcorn snack. On Sunday nights, I was famous for making fried okra and creamed corn sandwiches with fresh slices of tomato and loads of Duke's mayonnaise. Years later, while studying in Italy, I realized that Italians also took leftover vegetables and made sandwiches. All you need are cold vegetables, bread, and mayo.

The Caesar salad treatment makes this lighter than a sandwich, although if you want to give it more heft, you can add shrimp, chicken, or duck.

Makes 6 servings

2 cups Fried Okra (page 70)
2 heads romaine lettuce, leaves separated
1 cup cooked fresh corn kernels, chilled
2½ cups cubed corn bread, toasted
½ cup sliced grape tomatoes
½ cup sliced seedless cucumber
¼ cup sliced red onion
Creole Caesar Dressing (recipe follows)

Place half the fried okra in a large bowl and add the romaine, corn, corn bread, tomatoes, cucumber, and onion. Add the dressing and toss until well coated.

Divide the salad among six serving plates and top evenly with the remaining okra. Serve immediately.

Creole Caesar Dressing

Make about 1¼ cups

⅔ cup extra-virgin olive oil

3 garlic cloves, peeled

2 tablespoons chopped onion

2 tablespoons red wine vinegar

½ roasted red bell pepper

1 tablespoon finely chopped celery

1 teaspoon light brown sugar

¼ teaspoon cayenne pepper

2 tablespoons mayonnaise

¼ cup grated Parmesan cheese

Salt and pepper

In a small saucepan, combine the oil, garlic, and onion. Cook over low heat until the garlic and onion are golden and tender, about 15 minutes. Using a slotted spoon, transfer the garlic and onion to a food processor; reserve the oil.

Add the vinegar, bell pepper, celery, sugar, cayenne, mayonnaise, Parmesan, and a pinch each of salt and black pepper to the food processor. Pulse until smooth. With the machine running, add the oil in a thin stream and process until emulsified. Taste and season with salt and pepper. Use immediately or store in an airtight container in the refrigerator for up to 1 week.

Spicy Okra Shrimp Soup

This dish is soul in a bowl: the cure for what ails you, from hurt feelings to disappointment to desires unfulfilled. This is an easy, ready-in-30-minutes weeknight meal, but I love it even more as a weekend comfort dish. Cook a big pot of it on a Saturday, and the flavors will be even sweeter and deeper when you reheat it on Sunday afternoon.

Makes 6 servings

¼ cup olive oil

1 cup chopped onion

4 garlic cloves, minced

¼ cup chopped celery

¼ cup chopped green bell pepper

2½ pounds okra, trimmed and cut into bite-size pieces

3 bay leaves

2 teaspoons chopped fresh thyme

¼ cup tomato paste

4 cups canned diced tomatoes

3 cups clam juice or unsalted chicken stock

½ teaspoon cayenne pepper

1½ pounds medium shrimp, peeled, deveined, and chopped

Salt and pepper

Juice of 2 lemons

In a large saucepot, heat the oil over medium heat. Add the onion, garlic, celery, bell pepper, okra, bay leaves, and thyme. Cook, stirring often, until the okra is cooked through, about 5 minutes. Add the tomato paste and cook, stirring, until the paste really works itself into the mixture, about 5 minutes.

Add the diced tomatoes and stock and bring to a simmer over medium-high heat. Reduce the heat to low, cover, and simmer until the flavors come together, about 15 minutes.

Add the cayenne, shrimp, and a pinch each of salt and black pepper. Simmer until the shrimp are cooked through, 4 to 5 minutes.

Discard the bay leaves. Stir in the lemon juice. Taste, season with salt and black pepper, and serve.

Fried Okra

Nothing says "Southern" like the smell of okra frying in a cast-iron skillet atop an angry flame. Done right, everybody loves okra. I have been known to turn the most fervent okra haters into okra lovers. Herbs and spices and the right cooking techniques can really change the experience and flavor. As an adult, I grilled okra for the first time, and added it to hushpuppies that turned into okra fritters. I've made okra relish and—dare I say it—jalapeño-okra jam and okra dip. You tell me you don't like okra, then boy, do I have a few recipes for you (see pages 72, 73, and 109).

Makes 6 servings

1 pound okra, trimmed and halved lengthwise
¼ teaspoon cayenne pepper
Salt and pepper
1 cup buttermilk
Peanut, canola, or vegetable oil, for frying
½ cup fine white cornmeal
2 cups rice flour

Place the okra in a medium bowl. Season with the cayenne and salt and black pepper. Toss with the buttermilk until well coated and let sit for 10 to 15 minutes; drain well.

Fill a large cast-iron skillet with oil to a depth of ½ inch. Heat over medium-high heat to 350°F.

Combine the cornmeal, rice flour, ½ teaspoon salt, and ¼ teaspoon black pepper in a shallow dish. Dredge the okra in the cornmeal mixture, shaking off any excess. Working in batches to avoid crowding the skillet, add to the hot oil and fry, turning once, until golden brown, about 2 minutes per side. Drain on a crumpled brown paper bag or paper towels.

Serve immediately.

You tell me
you don't
like okra,
then boy,
do I have a
few recipes
for you.

Stewed Okra with Corn and Tomato

This dish was served in my grandparents' house for as long as I can remember. A real Low Country favorite, okra, corn, and tomato is like a great Broadway song, open to your interpretation. Try it simply seasoned with a slab of fatback or fresh smoked bacon. Try it with a little bit of hot pepper over a big pot of Carolina rice. My father would add shrimp, crabmeat, or fish to this dish. In our home, seafood was always preferred, and that made it akin to a big pot of gumbo.

Makes 6 servings

¼ cup olive oil

½ cup chopped onion

3 garlic cloves, sliced

1½ pounds okra, trimmed and halved lengthwise

2 cups grape tomatoes, halved

1 cup fresh corn kernels

Salt and pepper

In a large skillet, heat the oil over medium-high heat. Add the onion and garlic and cook, stirring often, until the onion is translucent, about 3 minutes. Increase the heat to high and add the okra. Cook, stirring often, until the okra is seared, about 3 minutes more. Stir in the tomatoes and corn and season with salt and pepper.

Cover, reduce the heat to low, and cook, stirring occasionally, until the flavors come together, about 15 minutes.

Taste, season with salt and pepper, and serve immediately.

Roasted Okra with Herbs, Pepper, and Garlic

The roasting in this recipe creates a crispy crust that is a nice alternative for those who want the taste of okra without the sticky texture.

Makes 6 servings

2 pounds okra, trimmed and halved lengthwise

¼ cup olive oil

¼ cup chopped fresh herbs (preferably a mixture of rosemary, sage, and thyme)

6 garlic cloves, chopped

Salt and pepper

Preheat the oven to 400°F.

In a large bowl, toss the okra, oil, herbs, garlic, and a pinch each of salt and pepper until the okra is well coated with the oil. Spread the okra over a half-sheet pan in a single layer.

Roast, tossing often, until the okra is cooked through, about 20 minutes. Serve hot.

This corn is so versatile. It makes an elegant side dish, a perfect predinner snack, or—and this is my favorite—a late-night supper with a flight of bourbon.

Broiled Sweet Corn with Tarragon-Cayenne Butter

My mother was what I call a "salt and pepper cook," meaning that while she seasoned food well, her cooking was a lot more Protestant. A few herbs here and there would do. A touch of garlic powder, celery, thyme or sage, and nutmeg and cinnamon on a sweet potato was as far as she would go.

My father's Geechee side of the family, the true Gullah folks, were a different breed. In a Smalls household, everything went in the pot, including a whole lot of spice and cayenne. We called that preheating: cayenne and *then* the hot sauce.

This corn is so versatile. It makes an elegant side dish, a perfect predinner snack, or—and this is my favorite—a late-night supper with a flight of bourbon.

Makes 6 servings

4 tablespoons (½ stick) unsalted butter, melted

¼ cup extra-virgin olive oil

1 tablespoon finely chopped fresh tarragon

½ teaspoon minced garlic

½ teaspoon cayenne pepper

Salt and pepper

6 ears corn, shucked

Position a rack 6 inches from the broiler heat source. Preheat the broiler.

In a medium bowl, mix the butter, oil, tarragon, garlic, cayenne, and a pinch each of salt and black pepper until well combined.

Place the corn on a half-sheet pan in a single layer. Brush with enough of the butter mixture to generously coat, reserving some of the mixture for serving. Broil the corn, turning often, until tender and lightly charred in spots, about 15 minutes.

Place the corn on a serving platter. Brush with the remaining butter mixture and serve.

Fried Sweet White Corn

I haven't boiled corn in decades. I simply have no interest in diluting its flavor. Not to mention that as a musician, the sizzle of corn hitting a cast-iron skillet is one of the most pitch-perfect sounds I know. What makes this dish unusual is the nutmeg, a note that I get from my mother. In addition to using nutmeg in sweet potato pie, pumpkin pie, and candied yams, Mom put a dash in her corn dishes. I love the taste.

Makes 6 servings

4 tablespoons (½ stick) unsalted butter
¼ cup chopped onion
4 cups fresh white corn kernels
¼ cup finely chopped green onions
¼ cup chopped fresh parsley
Salt and pepper
⅛ teaspoon ground nutmeg

In a medium skillet, melt the butter over medium heat. Add the onion and cook, stirring often, until translucent, about 4 minutes.

Add the corn, green onions, parsley, and a pinch each of salt and pepper. Cook, stirring often, until the corn is heated through and the green onions are tender, 5 to 6 minutes. Stir in the nutmeg and serve.

Fresh Creamed Corn Garnished with Crispy Leeks

As a kid, corn in season meant creamed corn every Sunday, with fried okra and big powdered biscuits. Creamed corn remains one of the top ten dishes I crave. I could eat it hot or cold, in a bowl, or smeared on a slice of bread or a toasted biscuit with thinly sliced tomatoes and, if I'm lucky, some fried okra and onions on top. This dish evokes home, comfort like a lullaby.

The first and only time I was ever served creamed corn from a can, the taste was so vile, I didn't recognize the dish. If that canned atrocity is what you grew up on, this recipe is how the universe begins to make amends.

Chef's tip: A great creamed corn starts with how you cut the corn from the cob. The biggest mistake people make is cutting the kernels whole, which gives the wrong texture to the dish. The trick is to slice off the tops of kernels, then scrape the cob with the knife to release the pulp and remaining bits. Done properly, this sets you up for success.

Makes 6 servings

(continued)

Fresh Creamed Corn Garnished with Crispy Leeks (*continued*)

Peanut, canola, or vegetable oil, for frying

2 cups julienned leeks

½ cup cornstarch

4 tablespoons (½ stick) unsalted butter

1 medium onion, chopped

1½ tablespoons all-purpose flour

1 cup heavy cream

½ cup whole milk

Salt and pepper

6 cups fresh corn kernels (see Chef's tip)

As a kid, corn in season meant creamed corn every Sunday, with fried okra and big powdered biscuits.

Fill a medium cast-iron skillet with oil to a depth of 1 inch. Heat over medium-high heat to 350°F.

In a large bowl, toss the leeks with the cornstarch, then shake off any excess. Add half the leeks to the hot oil and fry, turning occasionally, until golden brown and crisp, about 2 minutes. Drain on a crumpled brown paper bag or paper towels. Repeat with the remaining leeks.

In a medium saucepan, melt the butter over medium heat. Add the onion and cook, stirring often, until translucent, about 3 minutes. Add the flour and cook, stirring, until thick, about 3 minutes. Stir in the cream, milk, and a pinch each of salt and pepper. Cook, stirring, until thickened, about 5 minutes. Stir in the corn and cook, stirring, until the corn is heated through, 3 to 4 minutes.

Transfer the creamed corn to a bowl, garnish with the crispy leeks, and serve immediately.

Corn Catfish Soup with Bacon and Mint

In this dish, the bacon creates the base of savory needed to build bold flavor. It isn't essential to the dish, but once you have it with the chowder, you always want it. The mint is an ode to summer, and much like in many Asian dishes, the mint is a flavorful afterthought that adds a hit of freshness and tang, unexpected and complementary.

Makes 6 servings

4 (6-ounce) skinless catfish fillets

4 tablespoons olive oil

Salt and pepper

4 tablespoons (½ stick) unsalted butter

½ cup finely chopped onion

2 tablespoons finely chopped celery

¼ cup all-purpose flour

2½ quarts unsalted chicken stock

3 cups fresh corn kernels

1 cup heavy cream

¼ cup chopped fresh parsley

2 tablespoons chopped fresh mint

6 slices bacon, cooked until crisp and crumbled

Preheat the oven to 500°F.

Brush the catfish with 2 tablespoons of the oil and season with salt and pepper. Place the fish on a half-sheet pan in a single layer. Roast until the catfish is cooked through, about 10 minutes. Set aside until cool enough to handle, then flake the fish.

Meanwhile, in a large stockpot, melt the butter over medium heat. Add the remaining 2 tablespoons oil, the onion, and the celery. Cook, stirring often, until the onion is translucent, about 5 minutes. Add the flour and cook, stirring, until thick, about 5 minutes. Stir in the stock, corn, and cream and bring to a simmer.

Transfer 1 cup of the soup to a blender and puree until smooth (use caution when blending hot liquids). Return the pureed soup to the pot. Add the roasted catfish and the parsley. Taste and season with salt and pepper. Cook until the catfish is heated through, about 4 minutes.

Ladle into bowls, garnish with the mint and bacon, and serve immediately.

Sweet Pickle Potato Salad

Oh, honey. Where I come from, you were judged as a cook not on your soufflés but on your potato salad. They didn't give out actual blue ribbons, but having your potato salad be the talk of town was prize enough to inspire some pretty intense rivalries. As anyone who has tried and mastered this dish knows, it's a very basic recipe. What really distinguishes one salad from another is how the home cook navigates restraint and balance. Are you convinced that a dash of yellow mustard or a spoonful of minced onions will elevate your dish? Then go for it. Is your addition a hint of smoked paprika, or a handful of celery seeds that might be invisible to the naked eye but unmistakable on the palate? For me, the perfect balance of pickle relish made or broke the recipe. And I can say with pride that my friends have always rallied for my version of this Southern showstopper.

You can serve this as a starter with added protein such as shrimp or scallops. I also love it served alongside

(continued)

Sweet Pickle Potato Salad (*continued*)

a crab cake or crispy chicken livers. Leftovers can be spread thinly on a slice of bread and topped with a slab of smoked ham to make the most delicious sandwich. One note: The secret to my version of this dish is sweet pickle relish. Southern potato salad calls for sweet pickle relish, not diced cucumbers, dill pickles, or cornichons.

Makes 6 servings

1 pound small red potatoes, scrubbed

Salt and pepper

½ cup finely chopped onion

½ cup sweet pickle relish

½ cup mayonnaise

4 hard-boiled eggs (see page 14), finely chopped

Put the potatoes in a large pot and add enough cold water to cover them by 1 inch. Add a pinch of salt. Bring to a boil and cook until the potatoes are tender but not mushy, about 15 minutes. Drain. Set aside until cool enough to handle.

While the potatoes are still warm, cut them into quarters and place them in a large bowl. Add the onion, relish, mayonnaise, and eggs. Toss until well combined. Taste and season with salt and pepper.

Cover and chill until ready to serve, at least 1 hour or up to overnight.

Creole Potato Salad

What gives this salad that special Creole flavor is the holy trinity of Louisiana cooking: onions, bell peppers, and celery. I would also suggest a generous sprinkling of red pepper flakes if you've got the palate for spice.

Makes 6 servings

1 pound small red potatoes, scrubbed and halved

¼ cup olive oil

Salt and pepper

1½ cups steamed sugar snap peas

½ cup steamed fresh corn kernels

½ cup finely chopped onion

½ cup finely chopped celery

¼ cup minced green onions

¼ cup finely chopped red bell pepper

¼ cup sweet pickle relish

4 hard-boiled eggs (see page 14), chopped

½ cup mayonnaise

¼ cup minced fresh parsley

Preheat the oven to 400°F.

On a half-sheet pan, toss the potatoes with the oil until coated. Spread them in a single layer and season with salt and pepper. Roast until the potatoes are tender but not mushy, about 20 minutes.

Transfer the roasted potatoes to a large bowl and add the snap peas, corn, onion, celery, green onions, bell pepper, relish, eggs, mayonnaise, and parsley. Toss until well combined. Taste and season with salt and pepper. Serve warm.

Lemon Candied Yams

Lemon gives this dish an unexpected freshness, like a slice of lemon in an iced tea.

Chef's tip: Don't be afraid of the high oven heat used in this dish—you need high temps to give the yams that glorious steaklike sear.

Makes 6 servings

2½ pounds yams (about 4 large), peeled and cut into 1-inch cubes
8 tablespoons (1 stick) unsalted butter, melted
½ cup firmly packed light brown sugar
½ teaspoon ground cinnamon
½ teaspoon ground nutmeg
Zest and juice of 1 lemon
Salt and pepper

Preheat the oven to 400°F.

In a large bowl, toss the yams with the melted butter, brown sugar, cinnamon, nutmeg, lemon zest, and a pinch each of salt and pepper until evenly coated. Spread the yams in a single layer on a half-sheet pan. Roast until lightly caramelized, about 35 minutes.

Remove from the oven and immediately squeeze the juice from the lemon all over the yams. Serve hot.

Citrus-Whipped Sweet Potatoes

In her landmark cookbook *The Gift of Southern Cooking,* Edna Lewis recommends that "If you have any leftovers, try them cold the next day: they're a great mid-morning snack with a strong cup of coffee." It is a grand idea. The trouble is, whenever I make these citrus-whipped sweet potatoes, there are never any leftovers!

Makes 6 servings

2½ pounds sweet potatoes (about 4 large), scrubbed
½ cup heavy cream
¼ cup firmly packed dark brown sugar
4 tablespoons (½ stick) unsalted butter, softened
¼ teaspoon ground cinnamon
¼ teaspoon ground nutmeg
2 tablespoons fresh lemon zest
Salt

Preheat the oven to 375°F.

Place the sweet potatoes on a half-sheet pan. Bake until soft, about 1 hour; you should be able to drive a fork into them when they're done. Set aside until cool enough to handle. Reduce the oven temperature to 350°F.

Peel the sweet potatoes and place them in the bowl of a stand mixer fitted with the whisk attachment. Whip the potatoes on medium speed until mashed. Add the cream, brown sugar, butter, cinnamon, nutmeg, lemon zest, and a pinch of salt. Whip on medium speed until smooth.

Spread the mashed sweet potatoes into a shallow 2-quart baking dish.

Bake until firm and lightly browned on top, about 15 minutes. Serve warm.

Lady Lima Succotash Salad with Fresh Mint

This is a simple but grand dish. I love to serve it to international guests whose experience with American cuisine might be limited.

Lady Lima Succotash Salad with Fresh Mint (*continued*)

I have been eating succotash salad all my life. I wanted to own the dish and bring it home with a twist . . . What better way to do that than to marry the concept of lima beans, or what we in the South call succotash, with the succulent taste of crabmeat?

The dressing is a moment to create flavor. The heavy cream is for texture, the Champagne vinegar for taste.

This is a simple but grand dish. I love to serve it to international guests whose experience with American cuisine might be limited. This is almost always something they've never tasted before. How often can you say that?

Makes 6 servings

4 garlic cloves, unpeeled

6 ears corn, shucked

¼ cup plus 2 tablespoons extra-virgin olive oil

2 cups frozen lima beans

1 red bell pepper, chopped

1 yellow bell pepper, chopped

2 cups grape tomatoes, halved

½ cup chopped red onion

¼ cup minced fresh parsley

3 tablespoons sliced fresh mint

2 tablespoons Champagne vinegar

2 tablespoons heavy cream

¼ teaspoon sugar

Salt and pepper

Preheat the oven to 350°F.

Wrap the garlic in aluminum foil. Roast until soft, about 30 minutes. Set aside until cool enough to handle.

Meanwhile, heat a grill to medium-high.

Squeeze the roasted garlic between your fingertips to release the cloves; discard the papery skins and finely chop the cloves. Transfer to a large bowl.

Brush the corn with 2 tablespoons of the oil. Grill the corn, turning occasionally, until tender and charred in spots, about 13 minutes. Set aside until cool enough to handle, then cut the kernels from the cobs and add them to the bowl with the garlic.

Fill a medium bowl with ice and water. Bring a medium saucepan of water to a boil. Add the lima beans to the boiling water and cook until tender, 5 to 8 minutes. Drain and transfer to the ice water to cool. Drain the lima beans again and add them to the bowl with the corn.

Add the bell peppers, tomatoes, onion, parsley, mint, vinegar, cream, sugar, and remaining ¼ cup oil. Toss until evenly coated.

Taste and season with salt and black pepper. Cover and chill for at least 30 minutes or transfer to an airtight container and refrigerate for up to 2 days before serving.

Baked Spicy Barbecue Beans

The first "meal" I ever cooked was my stovetop version of baked beans: pork and beans with franks. I was five years old. This is my oven version of that humble dish. Spicy, tangy, and full of flavor, this is great as a snack or as a main course with your favorite hot dogs, grilled chicken, or steak. I have even been known to top my hot dog with these beans and a spoonful of Carolina Cabbage Slaw with Roasted Sweet Corn (page 61). These beans and a bowl of rice will make you happy, too.

Makes 6 servings

1 cup finely chopped onion

1 cup finely chopped celery

4 garlic cloves, finely chopped

4 cups cooked kidney beans

2 cups Carolina Bourbon Barbecue Sauce
    (see page 17)

2 tablespoons Tabasco sauce

Salt

1 cup chopped crispy bacon

½ teaspoon cayenne pepper

1 teaspoon cracked black pepper

Preheat the oven to 375°F.

In large cast-iron skillet, combine the onion, celery, and garlic and cook, stirring, until translucent or caramelized, about 15 minutes. Add the beans and cook, stirring frequently, for 5 minutes.

Pour the mixture into a 2-quart Dutch oven and add the barbecue sauce and Tabasco. Season with salt. Bake for 40 minutes. Remove from the oven.

Dust the bacon with the cayenne pepper and place on top of the beans. Sprinkle with cracked pepper, and serve.

Spicy Charleston Black Beans

For me, black beans are elegant and mysterious. From Asia to Latin America, black beans have been cooked in every possible way. You'll see them fermented for spicy sauces and in delicious colorful salads.

These beans will take you from season to season. (And don't be afraid of using canned beans if you're in a hurry.) In the wintertime, I pair them with roasted chicken, lamb chops, or a meat loaf with a serving of rice. In the summer, think grilled fish with a black bean side, or crispy skillet shrimp with black beans, extra benne seeds, and lots of red pepper flakes.

Makes 6 servings

4 garlic cloves, unpeeled

2 tablespoons olive oil

1½ cups chopped Vidalia onions

1 large red bell pepper, chopped

2 jalapeños, minced

1 teaspoon ground cumin

½ teaspoon chili powder

4 cups cooked black beans

4 ripe tomatoes, cored and chopped

1 tablespoon minced fresh cilantro

Salt and pepper

Preheat the oven to 350°F.

Wrap the garlic in aluminum foil. Roast until soft, about 30 minutes. Set aside until cool enough to handle, then squeeze the roasted garlic between your fingertips to release the cloves; discard the papery skins and chop the cloves.

In a medium saucepan, heat the oil over medium heat. Add the roasted garlic, onions, bell pepper, and jalapeños. Cook, stirring often, until the onions are translucent, about 4 minutes. Add the cumin, chili powder, and beans. Cook, stirring often, until the flavors come together, 4 to 5 minutes.

Add the tomatoes and cilantro and mix well. Taste and season with salt and pepper. Pour onto a platter and serve immediately.

Sautéed Green Beans with Toasted Charleston Benne Seeds

I love this dish year-round: warm as a side or chilled as the base of a salad. Just add fresh tomato and your favorite leafy herb—fresh mint and basil work especially well.

Chef's tip: In African cooking, sesame seeds are called benne seeds. They are used as both an ingredient and a seasoning or topping.

Makes 6 servings

2 tablespoons olive oil

1 tablespoon minced garlic

½ teaspoon finely chopped fresh thyme

½ teaspoon finely chopped fresh rosemary

1½ pounds green beans

¼ cup unsalted vegetable or chicken stock

Salt and pepper

1½ tablespoons toasted benne (white sesame) seeds

In a large saucepan, heat the oil, garlic, thyme, and rosemary over medium-high heat. When the garlic turns golden, add the green beans and cook, turning them with tongs, until they brighten in color, about 5 minutes. Add the stock, increase the heat to medium, and cover. Simmer, turning the beans occasionally, until tender, 3 to 4 minutes.

Taste and season with salt and pepper. Toss with the benne seeds and serve immediately.

Stewed Collard Greens with Smoked Turkey

Generally speaking, I steam, sauté, or wilt my greens, keeping that bright green coloring and leafy pull intact. But every now and then, I long for my mother's stewed greens: that big stainless-steel pot on the back burner, simmering with the weight of smoked ham. Her fresh collard greens bathed in that spicy stock for hours. To my impatient palate, it seemed like days. When I make this dish, I substitute smoked turkey or smoked chicken for the pork, and I braise the greens till tender. Try these wonderful greens on top of a bowl of steaming-hot rice or spicy noodles. Sometimes, when I'm feeling indulgent, I have them with grits swimming in butter with a side of corn bread.

Makes 6 servings

8 garlic cloves, unpeeled

8 tablespoons (1 stick) unsalted butter

1 cup chopped onion

6 pounds collard greens, tough stems discarded and leaves coarsely chopped

1 tablespoon chopped fresh herbs (preferably a mixture of rosemary, sage, and thyme)

1 large smoked turkey wing

¼ cup apple cider vinegar

6 cups unsalted chicken stock

Salt and pepper

(continued)

Stewed Collard Greens with Smoked Turkey *(continued)*

Try these wonderful greens on top of a bowl of steaming-hot rice or spicy noodles.

Preheat the oven to 350°F.

Wrap the garlic in aluminum foil. Roast until soft, about 30 minutes. Set aside until cool enough to handle, then squeeze the roasted garlic between your fingertips to release the cloves; discard the papery skins.

In a large stockpot, melt the butter over medium-high heat. Add the onion and cook, stirring occasionally, until translucent, about 5 minutes. Add the roasted garlic, collard greens, herbs, turkey wing, vinegar, and stock and bring to a boil. Reduce the heat to medium-low, cover, and simmer, stirring occasionally, until the greens are very soft, 35 to 40 minutes.

Discard the turkey wing. Taste, season with salt and pepper, and serve immediately

Pan-Fried Cabbage with Bacon

I love the leafiness of cabbage, infused with the scent and taste of cured bacon. For me, it speaks to family and the countryside. My mother steamed or stewed her cabbage, but my grandparents fried it. Grandpa would say that the cabbage was full of water and that adding water dilutes the flavor. Through the ages, both in African and African American cooking, everything happened in the stockpot or the frying pan. Braising or frying was always about flavor. When making this dish, I like adding flavors upon flavors. You can throw any leftovers into the pot: beans, corn, sweated tomatoes. I often toss in okra. Either way, it's delicious.

Makes 6 servings

¼ pound hickory-smoked slab bacon, cut into 1-inch chunks
2 tablespoons olive oil
2 heads savoy cabbage, cored and coarsely chopped
2 tablespoons apple cider vinegar
Salt and pepper

In a large pot, cook the bacon, covered, over medium-low heat until the fat renders, about 25 minutes. Uncover and cook, stirring occasionally, until crisp, about 5 minutes more. Drain all but 2 tablespoons of the fat from the pan.

Add the oil and cabbage to the pot and cook, stirring often, until wilted, about 5 minutes.

Stir in the vinegar. Taste, season with salt and pepper, and serve.

Herb-Sautéed Greens with Roasted Garlic and Turnips

I grew up eating turnip greens; they were my favorite greens. Traditionally, the turnip bottoms would be stewed with the greens. They were like vegetable dumplings I couldn't get enough of, and added so much flavor and texture. As a professional chef, I realized I could bring even more flavor to this family dish by roasting the bottoms separately, giving them a unique taste that complements the greens beautifully.

This is a true comfort dish for all occasions. I love to serve it on holidays: Thanksgiving, Christmas, as well as Easter Sundays with lamb or fish. Your guests will love it.

Makes 8 servings

3 cups cubed peeled turnips

3 tablespoons plus ¼ cup olive oil

Salt and pepper

½ cup garlic cloves, unpeeled

4 pounds collard greens, tough stems discarded and leaves coarsely chopped

3 pounds turnip greens, tough stems discarded and leaves coarsely chopped

¼ cup chopped fresh herbs (preferably a mixture of rosemary, sage, and thyme)

½ cup unsalted vegetable or chicken stock

Preheat the oven to 450°F.

On a half-sheet pan, toss the turnips with 2 tablespoons of the oil and a pinch each of salt and pepper. Roast until tender and toasted, about 30 minutes.

Place the garlic on a sheet of aluminum foil, drizzle with 1 tablespoon of the oil, and wrap well. Roast alongside the turnips until soft and golden brown, about 20 minutes. Set aside until cool enough to handle, then squeeze the roasted garlic between your fingertips to release the cloves; discard the papery skins.

Meanwhile, in a large pot, heat the remaining ¼ cup oil over medium heat. Add the collard and turnip greens by the fistful, stirring to coat the greens with the oil and adding more as they shrink. Stir in the herbs and stock, cover, and cook until the greens are just tender, about 10 minutes.

Add the turnips and roasted garlic. Taste and season with salt and pepper. Cover and cook until heated through, about 5 minutes more. Serve hot.

This is a true comfort dish for all occasions. I love to serve it on holidays: Thanksgiving, Christmas, as well as Easter Sundays with lamb or fish. Your guests will love it.

4.

Opera

Fish and Seafood

Summertime and the livin'
is easy.
Fish are jumping and the
cotton is high.
Oh yo' daddy's rich and yo'
ma is good looking.
So hush, little baby, don't
you cry.
—*"Summertime" from the
opera* Porgy and Bess

Although many do not know it, the roots of opera in the African American community run deep. In 1873, a group of African Americans formed Washington, D.C.'s first opera company, and performed *The Doctor of Alcantara* up and down the eastern seaboard. In 1892, Sissieretta Jones, the great soprano, performed at the White House. She would go on to perform for four American presidents and the British royal family. Each time she visited the White House, she was forced to walk in the back door until Theodore Roosevelt invited her through the front door.

For me, opera has always been synonymous with dreaming. Despite the precedent of singers like Jessye Norman and Leontyne Price, it was unusual in the 1950s to be a black boy in South Carolina dreaming of growing up to be an opera singer. My uncle Joe was a chef. He could also play the piano by ear. He couldn't read a note but could play almost anything. He gave me permission to dream and taught me that dreaming had power. He armed me with tools like Shakespeare, Wagner,

Puccini, and Verdi. It was a language I didn't speak with anybody but my uncle Joe.

In our modern age, the rich history of African American fishing communities remains as hidden as the history of African American opera singers. In port towns throughout the South, African American fishermen found a freedom and independence that farming life could never offer. The "Saturday Night Fish Fry," immortalized in song by the great Louis Jordan, was a celebration of how good life could be in these coastal cities and towns.

Porgy and Bess, the opera by George and Ira Gershwin, in its depiction of the fictionalized town of Catfish Row, brought the worlds of African American fishing communities and opera together. In my first job, with the Houston Grand Opera, I performed in *Porgy and Bess*, making my national and international debut as Jake, the young fisherman. It was the first complete version of every note that Gershwin wrote, and we received a Tony

For me,
opera has
always been
synonymous
with dreaming.

and a Grammy for the production and performance. The ballads we sang in that opera really summed up the life, work, and perils of fishing, but also the glory within—the courage and promised hope. I won a Grammy for my recording of *Porgy and Bess* with the Houston Grand Opera, so Catfish Row will always remain a special place for me.

As Henry Louis Gates Jr. once wrote, "I want to be black, to know black, to luxuriate in whatever I might be calling blackness at any particular time—but to do so in order to come out the other side, to experience a humanity that is neither colorless nor reducible to color. Bach and James Brown. Sushi and fried catfish." For me, *Porgy and Bess* is that touchstone that reminds me that I am neither colorless nor reducible to color. There is always, in my home, an aria waiting to be sung and Low Country feasts waiting to be eaten.

Fried Catfish Plate

Nothing says "Southern" like a plate of catfish. This crispy dish goes great with french fries, crispy baked fries, fried okra, and always with coleslaw. Fried catfish is also yummy with a red or brown gravy and some good old Carolina rice. Don't wait for Friday—have it anytime.

When cooking, make sure your pan is perfectly hot, but not too hot. If the oil is smoking, it's too hot, and you may have to start over with fresh oil. I like to test the oil by dropping in a piece of a vegetable (onion, celery) to see if the oil sizzles and agitates the vegetable. If the vegetable cooks evenly, I remove it and gently slide the fish into the pan.

Makes 6 servings

1 cup fine or medium white cornmeal

2 cups all-purpose flour

2 tablespoons garlic powder

1½ teaspoons celery seeds

1 tablespoon Old Bay seasoning

¼ teaspoon cayenne pepper

Salt and pepper

Peanut, canola, or vegetable oil, for frying

4 pounds skin-on catfish fillets

In a large bowl, whisk together the cornmeal, flour, garlic powder, celery seeds, Old Bay, cayenne, 1 teaspoon salt, and ½ teaspoon black pepper. Transfer to a large shallow dish.

Fill a large cast-iron skillet with oil to a depth of ¾ inch. Heat over medium-high heat to 350°F.

Sprinkle each side of the fish fillets with salt and pepper and then dredge in the cornmeal mixture. Shake off any excess. Working in batches to avoid crowding the skillet, slip the fillets into the hot oil and fry, turning once, until golden brown, about 2 minutes per side.

Drain on a crumpled brown paper bag or paper towels. Serve immediately.

Nothing says "Southern" like a plate of catfish.

Seared Grouper
with Spicy Gumbo Sauce

This dish combines the clean, light flavor of crispy seared fish with the "where y'at" flavor explosion of gumbo. If you have leftover gumbo, it'll taste just as good the next day over a bowl of rice.

Makes 6 servings

6 (5½-ounce) skinless grouper fillets
1 teaspoon cayenne pepper
Salt and pepper
2 cups all-purpose flour
¼ cup vegetable oil
Spicy Gumbo Sauce (recipe follows)

Line a half-sheet pan with parchment paper.

Season the grouper with the cayenne and salt and black pepper.

Put the flour in a large shallow dish and season it with ½ teaspoon salt and ¼ teaspoon black pepper. Dredge the grouper in the flour. Shake off any excess, then place the grouper on the prepared pan.

In a large skillet, heat the oil over medium-high heat. Working in batches, sear the grouper, carefully turning once, until golden brown and cooked through, about 4 minutes per side.

Transfer the grouper to a platter, ladle the sauce on top, and serve.

Spicy Gumbo Sauce

Makes about 1¾ cups

3 tablespoons olive oil

2 tablespoons all-purpose flour

¼ cup chopped onion

¼ cup chopped red bell pepper

¼ cup trimmed and sliced fresh okra

1 cup halved grape tomatoes

Juice of 1 lemon

½ cup fish stock

1 teaspoon minced habanero chile

Salt and pepper

In a medium saucepan, heat the oil over medium-high heat. Add the flour, reduce the heat to medium-low, and cook, stirring, until lightly browned, about 10 minutes.

Add the onion, bell pepper, okra, tomatoes, lemon juice, stock, and chile. Season with salt and black pepper, stir well, and bring to a simmer over medium heat. Reduce the heat to medium-low, cover, and cook until the vegetables are tender and the sauce thickened, about 15 minutes. Serve hot.

Shrimp and Okra Creole Sauté

My uncle James was the king of this dish and I just loved it. He and Aunt Mildred had two kids much younger than me, and when I was asked to babysit, my one requirement was having this dish be on the stove for my dinner while they were out. He would render the fat of salted pork and slowly add the ingredients, frying and steaming everything to perfection. He always served the sauté with a pot of rice or grits.

Making this dish as a chef, I add a few more ingredients than he ever would. As with all my dishes, I encourage you to make it your own: experiment with flavor and texture. Once you have the basics and feel like you own the dish, feel free to try new things: favorite aromatics like ginger and turmeric, crumbled bacon or ground sausage, or even extra garlic or soy sauce for that salty finish. Whatever you enjoy, add it.

Makes about 6 servings

¼ cup olive oil

1½ pounds okra, trimmed and cut into ½-inch-wide pieces

2½ teaspoons minced garlic

1 pound peeled and deveined large shrimp

1 cup halved grape tomatoes

½ cup chopped red bell pepper

½ cup chopped onion

½ cup minced fresh cilantro

1 teaspoon chopped fresh thyme

½ teaspoon rubbed sage

Salt and pepper

In a large heavy-bottomed skillet, heat the oil over medium-high heat. Add the okra and garlic. Cook, stirring occasionally, until the okra begins to soften, about 5 minutes.

Add the shrimp, tomatoes, bell pepper, onion, cilantro, thyme, and sage. Reduce the heat to medium. Season with salt and black pepper. Cook, stirring occasionally, until the shrimp are cooked through, about 5 minutes. Serve immediately.

Frogmore Stew

The first time I had this dish, I made it. I remember creating this dish for my third restaurant, Shoebox Café. The idea of it for me was the embodiment of a chowder-style Southern fish stew. I wanted a hearty dish that screamed "Southern," with a sophisticated twist.

Makes 8–10 servings

12 to 14 cups water, fish stock, or seafood stock

4 bay leaves

¼ cup plus 2 tablespoons Old Bay seasoning

1 cup chopped celery

1 cup chopped onions

½ cup whole peeled garlic cloves

3 whole bird's-eye chiles

1 pound small red potatoes, scrubbed, or 6 purple yams, cut into 2-inch chunks

1 pound smoked hot sausage links or chicken sage sausage, cut into 2-inch pieces

6 ears corn, shucked and quartered

2 pounds shell-on large shrimp

2 pounds shelled scallops

1 cup dry white wine

Salt and pepper

Coarsely chopped fresh cilantro, for garnish

In a large stockpot, combine 12 cups of the water or stock, the bay leaves, Old Bay, celery, onions, garlic, and chiles and bring to a boil over high heat. Add the potatoes and cook until tender, about 15 minutes.

Add the sausage and cook until heated through, about 5 minutes. Add the corn and cook until just tender, about 3 minutes. Stir in the shrimp, scallops, and wine and cook until the shrimp are cooked through, about 4 minutes. Season with salt and pepper and pour the stew into a large serving bowl. For more casual gatherings, serve directly from the pot on the stove. Garnish each serving with cilantro and serve immediately.

I wanted a hearty dish that screamed "Southern," with a sophisticated twist.

Sherry She-Crab Soup

This dish, for me, means family. When my father (I called him Da) and grandfather would return from the "Old Country" (which is what my sisters and I called the Low Country: Charleston, Beaufort, and the Gullah Islands), they'd arrive with crates of live crab, oysters, shrimp, and oversized grouper. The sound of Da's car in the driveway was a call to the kitchen, all hands on deck. It was a race against the clock: all that fresh seafood had to be prepped for eating or for storing in one of the big deep freezers in the pantry off the kitchen.

Mother would cook and prep to store the food simultaneously, while my dad, sisters and I worked hard to keep up with her. In between shucking oysters, cleaning shrimp, and picking crab, Mom would boil shells for stock and heat and stir hot milk for chowder and soup. She-crab soup was my favorite. With a generous pour of sherry, fresh lump

Don't be afraid to add extra crabmeat or freshly ground black pepper. I like a nice pinch of nutmeg, which comes to life, dancing in the creamy broth.

crabmeat, and hot sauce, passing the piping-hot bowls around the table was so much fun. Mother's soup was always one pot of luxurious goodness that we shared as a family.

For me, the secret of this dish is generosity. Don't be afraid to add extra crabmeat or freshly ground black pepper. I like a nice pinch of nutmeg, which comes to life, dancing in the creamy broth. Lots of eggs are also good, and a hit of ginger, too. Try it!

Makes 6 servings

(continued)

Sherry She-Crab Soup (*continued*)

8 tablespoons (1 stick) unsalted butter

¾ cup all-purpose flour

1 cup finely chopped onion

¼ cup finely chopped celery

3 garlic cloves, minced

1 cup clam juice

2 quarts whole milk

2 cups heavy cream

¼ cup Worcestershire sauce

3 pounds lump crabmeat, picked over for shells

1 cup cream sherry

¼ teaspoon ground nutmeg

Salt and pepper

6 hard-boiled quail eggs, halved

Hot sauce (optional)

In a large stockpot, melt the butter over medium-low heat. Add the flour and cook, whisking, until the flour loses its rawness but doesn't take on color, about 5 minutes. Add the onion, celery, and garlic. Cook, stirring, until tender, about 10 minutes.

Stir in the clam juice, milk, and cream and bring to a simmer. Reduce the heat to low, cover, and cook, stirring occasionally, until creamy, about 15 minutes.

Add the Worcestershire, crabmeat, sherry, and nutmeg. Season with salt and pepper. Cook, stirring occasionally, until the crab is heated through, about 5 minutes.

Serve hot, garnished with the quail eggs. Add hot sauce, if you like, to taste.

5.

Opening
Night Dishes:
Meat and
Chicken

Divas

We called this chapter "Divas." These are the big plates of the book, the high notes that a home cook can serve with pride, that tell a full story on the plate. Anyone who's cooked a fancy meal for company knows that there's an element of performance from beginning to end. I rarely sing onstage anymore, but these days an exceptional big pot of shrimp gumbo followed by a deep-dish sweet potato pie evokes the same kind of passion and joy.

Diva has become shorthand for a temperamental (most often female) singer with supersize talents and supersize tantrums to match. But that's not the kind a diva I'm talking about. I'm talking about the divas who really know how to put on a show. The ones who train and prepare for years before their big break because they live in service of the song.

A diva is a diva because average is simply not part of her repertoire; ordinary is not a language she is fluent in. As Tina Turner famously purred in the prelude to "Proud Mary," "I think you might like to hear something nice and easy, but there's just one thing, you see . . . We never ever do nothing nice and easy."

A diva is surprising, occasionally shocking, but never so-so. I dare say the same could be said about these recipes. These entrées are adorned with a dramatic but elegant dressing of indulgent sauces: gravies and glazes and such add glitter and grand notes to any meal, the aria your guests have been waiting for with anticipation.

These are diva dishes because the first time you attempt to make a true Southern fried chicken, you best be prepared to get a little sweat on your brow. A little "Patti LaBelle/Aretha Franklin/Mariah Carey hitting five octaves"-style sweat. A prime rib with crawfish gravy is not a "Let me roll out of bed on a Sunday around noon and have a dozen people come for supper around four" kind of meal. To paraphrase Debbie Allen's famous line from the iconic movie *Fame*, if you want flavors

These are diva dishes because the first time you attempt to make a true Southern fried chicken, you best be prepared to get a little sweat on your brow.

upon flavors, it's gonna cost you a little something. These dishes require more effort but the rewards are equally great.

If you're vegetarian, vegan, or simply looking for more vegetable-forward options, you can play with substituting tofu, seitan, and your favorite vegetables in place of these proteins. Your kitchen is your stage. And if you're good enough, you can steal a recipe just like a singer can steal a song. Nobody could break a heart quite like Otis Redding, but Aretha Franklin took *his* song, "Respect" and gave it a woman's touch, and it was never really an Otis song again. In this collection of diva recipes, I encourage you to steal, improvise, and make every recipe your own.

Roast Quail
in Bourbon Cream Sauce

I love quail. It's a sweet, succulent bird, very lean, its flavor concentrated, that's very popular in the South. Though it's often deep-fried in the Carolinas, I like it roasted, grilled, or sautéed, having first been dressed, semi-deboned, and marinated for a more complex flavor. Quail looks like a very small chicken, and is great as an appetizer, in a salad, or as a main course but you will need at least two of them, as they are petite. The taste is more pronounced than chicken but not as strong as turkey.

Aside from just being plain good, the bourbon cream sauce makes it Southern, the final affirmation that you are about to dine on an indulgent Southern delicacy. The cream sauce is very much influenced by my travels and studies in Europe, particularly in the early eighties while studying with my coach from the Paris Opera House. The cream sauces were a personal indulgence for me, and fowl is the perfect protein to create something so decadent.

Makes 6 servings

(continued)

Marinade

⅓ cup olive or mustard oil

Zest of 1 orange

Zest of 1 lime

4 cups pineapple juice

2 tablespoons fresh lime juice

1 tablespoon honey

⅓ cup soy sauce

1 tablespoon garlic

1 teaspoon cayenne pepper

1 teaspoon salt

1 teaspoon ground turmeric

1 teaspoon grated fresh ginger or ground ginger

12 semi-boneless quail, at room temperature

12 tablespoons (1½ sticks) unsalted butter, softened

3 tablespoons chopped fresh parsley

Salt and pepper

Bourbon Cream Sauce (recipe follows)

In a large nonmetallic bowl, mix together the oil, orange zest, lime zest, pineapple juice, lime juice, honey, soy sauce, garlic, cayenne, salt, turmeric, and ginger.

Rinse the quail and pat dry. Add them to the bowl with the marinade and cover. Refrigerate for at least 4 hours or up to 12 hours.

When ready to cook the quail, preheat the oven to 450°F.

Remove the quail from the marinade and pat dry with paper towels. Rub the quail all over with the butter and parsley and season with salt and black pepper. Place on a half-sheet pan.

Roast, basting often with the buttery pan juices, until the quail are golden brown, about 25 minutes.

Transfer to a platter and drizzle with the Bourbon Cream Sauce. Serve.

Bourbon Cream Sauce

Makes about 2 ½ cups

3 tablespoons olive oil

¼ cup finely chopped onion

2 garlic cloves, minced

2 tablespoons minced fresh tarragon

½ cup dry white wine

1 cup unsalted chicken stock

¾ cup heavy cream

½ cup bourbon

Salt and pepper

In a medium saucepan, heat the oil over medium heat. Add the onion and cook, stirring occasionally, until translucent, about 5 minutes. Add the garlic and cook, stirring often, until golden, about 3 minutes.

Add the tarragon, wine, and stock and bring to a simmer. Cook until reduced by one-fourth.

Add the cream and bourbon. Season with salt and pepper. Cook, stirring occasionally, until creamy, about 5 minutes. Use hot. Leftover sauce can be stored in the refrigerator for up to 4 days.

Free-Range Duck *with Creole Sauce*

If you are a connoisseur of dark meat chicken, duck is truly worthy of your curiosity. Duck is perfect for the Southern table. It represents the bounty of a great hunt, and freshly raised farm fowl dresses a Southern dinner or celebration in a grand way. The flavor is rich—a cross between chicken and veal, I like to say. Duck is a hearty fowl.

Chef's tip: Don't overcook the duck breast! It becomes dry and tough.

Makes 6 servings

6 skin-on, boneless free-range duck breast halves
    (about 2 pounds)
3 tablespoons rubbed sage
Salt and pepper
3 tablespoons olive oil
Creole Sauce (recipe follows)

Preheat the oven to 400°F.

Using a sharp knife, score the skin on each duck breast in a diamond crosshatch pattern. Rub with the sage and season with salt and pepper.

In a large skillet, heat the oil over high heat. Working in batches to avoid crowding the skillet, sear the duck, skin-side down, until the skin browns and the fat renders, 8 to 10 minutes. Transfer, skin-side up, to a half-sheet pan. Add 1 tablespoon of the fat from the skillet to the pan.

Roast until a meat thermometer inserted into the thickest part of the breast registers 135°F for medium-rare, 15 to 20 minutes. Let the duck rest for 10 minutes before slicing.

While the duck rests, in a medium saucepan, bring the Creole Sauce to a simmer over medium-low heat.

Slice the duck, fan the slices out on a serving platter, and drizzle with the warm sauce. Serve immediately.

Duck is
perfect for
the Southern
table.

Creole Sauce

Makes about 1½ cups

2 tablespoons olive oil

¼ cup finely chopped onion

3 garlic cloves, minced

1 red bell pepper, diced

¼ cup diced celery

1½ cups canned diced tomatoes

¼ cup apple cider vinegar

Juice of 2 lemons

1 tablespoon light brown sugar

2 tablespoons tomato paste

¼ teaspoon cayenne pepper

Salt and pepper

In a medium saucepan, heat the oil over medium-high heat. Add the onion, garlic, bell pepper, and celery. Cook, stirring occasionally, until the onion is translucent, 4 to 5 minutes.

Stir in the diced tomatoes, vinegar, lemon juice, brown sugar, tomato paste, and cayenne. Bring to a light boil. Reduce the heat to low, cover, and simmer until thickened but not stiff, about 15 minutes. It should have the consistency of a gravy. Taste and season with salt and black pepper. Use hot. Leftover sauce can be stored in the refrigerator for up to 4 days.

Oven-Fried Baby Chickens
with Hot Mustard–Apricot Jam Glaze

This dish stems from my love of jam and spicy sauce. Before I used this sauce on my chicken, I would spread it on toast. Creating this dish, I realized I loved the idea of crispy chicken skin glazed in a spicy jam mustard, so I made it happen.

This is a crispy roast chicken, perfect for a casual supper or a heavy weekend lunch. The recipe is all about ease: I wanted to achieve that fried-chicken flavor without all the deep-frying and oil. I also wanted to do this without having to stand in front of a skillet for the better part of an hour frying chicken.

Chef's tip: For this recipe, feel free to use other jams. I would recommend pineapple, peach, or a marmalade. I felt the apricot married well with the mustard. The taste is more neutral, and the fruit is firm and mild.

Makes 6 servings

3 whole (1-pound) Cornish game hens or poussins (baby chickens)

2 cups buttermilk

1 tablespoon garlic powder

1 tablespoon onion powder

1 tablespoon cayenne pepper

1 teaspoon sweet paprika

Salt and pepper

3½ cups all-purpose flour

Olive oil spray

Hot Mustard–Apricot Jam Glaze (recipe follows)

(continued)

**Oven-Fried Baby Chickens with
Hot Mustard–Apricot Jam Glaze** (*continued*)

Rinse the hens and pat dry with paper towels. Place them in a large bowl and add the buttermilk, garlic powder, onion powder, cayenne, paprika, ½ teaspoon salt, and ¼ teaspoon pepper. Cover and chill for at least 2 hours or up to overnight.

When ready to cook the hens, preheat the oven to 375°F. Line two half-sheet pans with parchment paper.

Put the flour in a large bowl and season with ¼ teaspoon each salt and pepper. Dredge the hens in the seasoned flour, shake off any excess, and place them on the prepared pans. Spray the hens generously with olive oil spray.

Bake until golden brown, about 40 minutes. When a knife is inserted into the meat, the juices should run clear.

Let the chicken rest for 10 minutes, generously glaze, and serve.

Before I used this sauce on my chicken, I would spread it on toast.

Hot Mustard–Apricot Jam Glaze

Makes about 2¼ cups

1 cup apricot preserves
1 cup hot mustard
¼ cup honey
1 tablespoon apple cider vinegar
Salt

In a blender, combine the preserves, mustard, honey, vinegar, and a pinch of salt and puree until smooth. Taste and season with salt. Use immediately or store in an airtight container in the refrigerator for up to 1 month.

Nikki Giovanni's brilliant poem describes why traditional African American food is as rich with meaning as it is with flavor. With her kind permission, we share this excerpt from her poem here.

"Quilting the Black-Eyed Pea (We're Going to Mars)"

When we go to Mars . . . it's the same thing . . . it's Middle
  Passage

When the rocket red glares the astronauts will be able to see
themselves pull away from Earth . . . as the ship goes deeper
they will see a sparkle of blue . . . and then one day not only will
they not see Earth . . . they won't know which way to look . . .
and that is why NASA needs to call Black America

They need to ask us: How did you calm your fears . . . How
were you able to decide you were human even when everything
said you were not . . . How did you find the comfort in the face
of the improbable to make the world you came to your world . . .
How was your soul able to look back and wonder

And we will tell them what to do: To successfully go to Mars
and back you will need a song . . . take some Billie Holiday for
the sad days and some Charlie Parker for the happy ones but
always keep at least one good spiritual for comfort . . . You
will need a slice or two of meatloaf and if you can manage it
some fried chicken in a shoebox with a nice moist lemon pound
cake . . . a bottle of beer because no one should go that far without a beer and maybe a six-pack so that if there is life on Mars
you can share . . . Popcorn for the celebration when you land
while you wait on your land legs to kick in . . . and as you climb
down the ladder from your spaceship to the Martian surface . . .
look to your left . . . and there you'll see a smiling community
quilting a black-eyed pea . . . watching you descend

—Nikki Giovanni

Southern Fried Chicken Plate

There's a lot to love in the memories of fried chicken.

Southern Fried Chicken Plate (*continued*)

A combination of West African batter frying in palm oil and Scottish flour frying in animal fat is how we arrived at the recipe for fried chicken that is prevalent today. Fried Chicken was a Southern dish that traveled from the African American communities to main street White America.

Some say that the negative stereotypes about black people and fried chicken can be traced to D. W. Griffith's 1915 film *Birth of a Nation*. Many of these images were a direct parallel to Jim Crow images and ignorant impressions that belittled us and compromised our dignity. Even though we loved fried chicken and all the great dishes that went with it, there was the impression that by eating it, you were supporting the less-than-favorable concept White America had created for you. Shame is the gift that keeps on giving, from slavery to racism and discrimination.

But when you step away from the stereotypes, there's a lot to love in the memories of fried chicken. In the days when blacks couldn't eat at every restaurant, black folks who traveled packed themselves a "shoebox lunch." I dare say there isn't a Southerner alive born before 1960 who didn't know someone who always made one. I love my version, served high or low: on silver platters or a picnic blanket, this is a dish that's bound to satisfy.

Makes 6 servings

2 (3-pound) chickens, each cut into 8 pieces

2 cups buttermilk

1 tablespoon garlic powder

1 tablespoon onion powder

1 tablespoon cayenne pepper

1 teaspoon sweet paprika

Salt and pepper

Peanut, canola, or vegetable oil, for frying

3½ cups all-purpose flour

Rinse the chicken pieces and pat dry with paper towels. Place them in a large bowl and add the buttermilk, garlic powder, onion powder, cayenne, paprika, ½ teaspoon salt, and ¼ teaspoon black pepper. Cover and chill for at least 2 hours or up to overnight.

Fill a large cast-iron skillet with enough oil to come halfway up the sides. Heat over medium-high heat to 350°F.

Put the flour in a large bowl and season with ¼ teaspoon each salt and pepper. Dredge the chicken pieces in the seasoned flour, shaking off any excess. Working in batches to avoid crowding the skillet, place the chicken in the hot oil and fry until golden brown on the bottom, 8 to 10 minutes. Turn the pieces carefully and fry until golden brown on the second side and cooked through, 5 to 6 minutes. Larger pieces may need a few more minutes of cooking time.

Drain on a crumpled brown paper bag or paper towels. Serve immediately.

Alexander's "Chase the Blues Away" Hot Dogs

I love a delicious chili dog with a generous heaping of cold slaw. This is my own unique "Happy Meal." I could eat a hot dog every day of my life and still long for more. I am very particular about my dogs. I have spent years researching the perfect frankfurters or wieners. Size, texture, and cooking technique are all important—as well as the quality and preparation of the bun.

I like a veal frank with natural casing, the chili made from ground beef or chicken, sautéed with onions, celery bits or celery seeds, and garlic; infused with chili powder, a mixture of cumin, peppers, imported smoked paprika, ketchup, and Worcestershire sauce; finished with fresh cilantro and simmered for 15 to 30 minutes . . . depending on how hungry you are.

This is such a fun meal to share with friends. Some years ago I gave myself a big birthday party and decided it would be a hot dog party. I was already famous for my "hot dog get-togethers," casual fun times perfectly suited for sharing franks and buns, so my friends were not shocked. Large silver-plated chaffing dishes were the centerpieces and container for my prized gourmet hot dogs, which were perfectly paired with martinis and pitchers of mint julep.

8 to 10 hot dogs

Chili Sauce
1 pound ground beef or ground chicken
¼ cup chopped white onion
1 tablespoon vegetable oil
1 cup beef or chicken stock
1 teaspoon chopped garlic
1 tablespoon chili powder
½ teaspoon ground cumin
½ teaspoon garlic powder
½ teaspoon onion powder
¼ teaspoon celery seeds
½ teaspoon pepper
½ teaspoon cayenne pepper
1 tablespoon dark brown sugar
¼ teaspoon salt
¼ teaspoon fresh or dried thyme
1 tablespoon Worcestershire sauce

1 teaspoon unsalted tomato paste

½ cup ketchup

6 to 8 beef or chicken hot dogs

6 to 8 wheat or potato buns, steamed

Carolina Cabbage Slaw (page 61)

Shredded cheese, jalapeños, pickle relish, and/or chopped onions, for serving (optional)

1½ teaspoons chopped fresh cilantro

For the chili sauce: In a large saucepan or deep-dish skillet, combine the ground beef or chicken, onion, and oil and heat over medium-high heat, stirring and breaking the meat up as it cooks, until the meat is almost cooked through, about 5 minutes. If using ground beef, add ⅓ cup of the stock; if using ground chicken, add ½ cup of the stock.

In a small bowl, stir together the garlic, chili powder, cumin, garlic powder, onion powder, celery seeds, black pepper, cayenne, brown sugar, salt, and thyme. Sprinkle the mixture evenly over the meat and cook, stirring, until the spice mixture is incorporated and the stock has been absorbed.

Add the Worcestershire and tomato paste and stir evenly. Add the ketchup and continue to stir. If the chili looks too thick, add the remaining stock.

Bring the chili to a gentle boil. Reduce the heat to medium, cover, and simmer for 15 to 20 minutes.

Meanwhile, boil the hot dogs.

When fully cooked, place each hot dog in the bun of your choice and garnish with Carolina Cabbage Slaw (page 61). Stir the cilantro into the chili or sprinkle it over the assembled hot dogs before serving.

This is such a fun meal to share with friends.

Roasted Stuffed Turkey
with Corn Bread–Chestnut Dressing

Corn bread stuffing dates back to slavery times. My chestnut stuffing is inspired by the amazing smell of "chestnuts roasting..." as Nat King Cole sings in "The Christmas Song." The aroma of those open-fired nuts combined with corn bread, sage, thyme, and a hint of bay leaf is magical and will invoke joy before your guests have even had their first bite.

Makes 8 to 10 servings

1 (10- to 12-pound) fresh turkey, giblets removed
8 tablespoons (1 stick) unsalted butter, cut into
   ¼-inch-thick pieces, softened
Salt and pepper
Corn Bread–Chestnut Dressing (recipe follows)

Preheat the oven to 350°F. Set a rack in a roasting pan.

Rinse the turkey inside and out and pat dry. Slide the butter pieces under the skin of the turkey breast and sides to generously coat the meat. Season the turkey all over with salt and pepper. Stuff the cavity with the dressing, truss, and place it on the rack.

Roast until a meat thermometer inserted into the thickest part of the thigh registers 180°F, about 2½ hours. Let rest for 15 minutes before transferring the dressing to a serving dish and carving the turkey.

Serve hot, with the dressing on the side.

Variation

Mix ¼ cup cane syrup with 4 tablespoons (½ stick) whipped or softened unsalted butter. Add ½ teaspoon ground cinnamon, ¼ teaspoon cayenne pepper, and ½ teaspoon orange zest. Mix well and spread over the hot turkey before serving.

Corn Bread–Chestnut Dressing

Makes about 6 cups

8 tablespoons (1 stick) unsalted butter

¼ cup finely chopped onion

½ cup finely chopped celery

1½ tablespoons rubbed sage

3 bay leaves

1 teaspoon chopped fresh thyme

12 ounces peeled roasted chestnuts, chopped

5 cups cubed corn bread

½ cup unsalted chicken stock

2 large eggs, beaten

¼ teaspoon ground nutmeg

Salt and pepper

In a large stockpot, melt the butter over medium heat. Add the onion, celery, sage, bay leaves, and thyme. Cook, stirring often, until the onion is translucent, 4 to 5 minutes. Reduce the heat to low.

Fold in the chestnuts, corn bread, stock, eggs, nutmeg, and a pinch each of salt and pepper. Let cool slightly before stuffing the dressing into the turkey.

Pan-Fried Rabbit with Root Vegetables and Redeye Gravy

Growing up in a Low Country household, my family ate rabbit. We dined on smothered rabbit, served in the most flavorful caramelized onion gravy, made with a dash of my grandfather's wild cherry wine, which he added to the pot to balance the gamey taste. While I did find it delicious, it would take me years to reconcile eating those cute bunnies that we bought dyed at Eastertime or the ones who appeared in my favorite cartoons with the rabbit in the pot. It wasn't until I began traveling in Europe as a young opera singer that I gave myself permission to again approach the dish with newfound sophistication and a sense of adventure. I remember dining on rabbit, served with heirloom vegetables swimming in a cream Calvados sauce, in a French restaurant with great delight.

This dish, for me, is an ode to my heritage, to all those fellow Southerners who hunt the land and in their own way have elevated the narrative and legacy of rabbit as an American dish.

(continued)

Chef's tip: **Wild rabbit is considered the best tasting and leanest variety. Marinate or brine the meat in your favorite marinade to neutralize the gaminess.**

Makes 4–6 servings

½ pound turnips, peeled and cut into 1-inch pieces

½ pound parsnips, peeled and cut into 1-inch pieces

½ pound yams, peeled and cut into 1-inch pieces

½ pound small red potatoes, scrubbed and cut into 1-inch pieces

2 leeks, cut into rounds

1 tablespoon fresh thyme leaves

1 tablespoon fresh rosemary leaves

5 whole peeled garlic cloves

¼ cup plus 3 tablespoons olive oil

Salt and pepper

¾ cup strong brewed coffee

¼ cup heavy cream

⅛ teaspoon ground nutmeg

2 tablespoons duck fat

4–5 pounds of bone-in rabbit pieces

1 teaspoon cayenne pepper

Preheat the oven to 400°F.

In a large bowl, mix the turnips, parsnips, yams, potatoes, and leeks. Add the thyme, rosemary, garlic, ¼ cup of the oil, and a pinch each of salt and black pepper. Mix well and spread over the bottom of a roasting pan in a single layer.

Roast until golden brown and tender, 45 to 50 minutes. Transfer the pan to the stovetop and set over high heat. Pour the coffee and cream into the pan and bring to a boil. Cook, stirring and scraping the pan with a wooden spoon, until the glazed bits are released from the pan, about 3 minutes. Reduce the heat to low, stir in the nutmeg, and simmer until thickened, about 2 minutes. Transfer the vegetables and gravy to a platter.

In a large skillet, heat the duck fat and remaining 3 tablespoons oil over medium-high heat. Season the rabbit with the cayenne and salt and black pepper. Working in batches, add the rabbit and sear, turning once, until browned and cooked through, about 7 minutes per side.

Set the rabbit over the roasted vegetables and gravy on the platter and serve.

Marinated Venison Roast
with Ginger-Berry Glaze

Marinated Venison Roast with Ginger-Berry Glaze (*continued*)

I love a venison meat loaf, and a venison roast is merely a fancier version. The berry glaze is traditional, but the ginger offers a slightly global twist, a nod to the Asian and Caribbean flavors that have crisscrossed with the African diaspora.

Makes 6 servings

1 (2½-pound) whole venison tenderloin, trimmed
1 large onion, sliced
6 garlic cloves, chopped
¼ cup olive oil
¼ cup Worcestershire sauce
Salt and pepper
Ginger-Berry Glaze (recipe follows)

Place the venison in a roasting pan.

In a medium bowl, combine the onion, garlic, oil, Worcestershire, and a pinch each of salt and pepper. Pour the mixture over the meat and thoroughly rub it into the meat. Cover and chill overnight.

When ready to cook the venison, preheat the oven to 375°F.

Roast the venison to your desired doneness. For medium-rare, roast until a meat thermometer inserted into the center of the meat registers 125°F, about 40 minutes. During the last 15 minutes of roasting, baste with the glaze every 5 minutes. Let the roast rest for 20 minutes so the juices can collect themselves before their debut.

Slice and serve with the pan juices.

Ginger-Berry Glaze

This glaze would work just as well with lamb, chicken, or even shrimp.

Makes about 3 cups

2½ cups raspberry preserves

¼ cup firmly packed dark brown sugar

2 teaspoons dry mustard

2 tablespoons ketchup

3 tablespoons apple cider vinegar

¼ cup chopped candied ginger

In a medium saucepan, mix the raspberry preserves, brown sugar, mustard, ketchup, vinegar, and ¼ cup water. Bring to a boil over medium heat and simmer, stirring occasionally, until thickened, about 10 minutes. Remove sauce from the stove, add candied ginger, and stir.

Use immediately or let cool and store in an airtight container in the refrigerator for up to 1 month.

Citrus-Glazed Pork Loin Roast
with Corn Cream Sauce

Because my father worked for a grocery company, we were exposed to all kinds of foods and cuts of meats. A pork loin roast rarely made the Sunday table, but any other day, Mother might find time to cook and serve it for a weekday dinner, usually with a pan gravy, but now and then with a sweet dried fruit glaze.

Chef's tip: This is a very successful dish, provided the meat is not overcooked. Because loin roast is a lean cut, overcooking it can render it dry and tasteless.

Makes 8 to 10 servings

1 (8-pound) bone-in pork loin roast, trimmed of
    excess fat
¼ cup olive oil
Salt and pepper
¼ cup Dijon mustard
¼ cup pure maple syrup or sorghum syrup
1 tablespoon chopped fresh rosemary
1 tablespoon lemon zest
1 tablespoon orange zest
Corn Cream Sauce (recipe follows)

Preheat the oven to 400°F. Line a roasting pan with aluminum foil and fit it with a rack.

Rub the pork with the oil and season with salt and pepper. Place the pork in the prepared pan. Roast until a brown crust forms, about 30 minutes.

Reduce the oven temperature to 325°F. Roast the pork, basting it with the pan juices every 15 to 20 minutes, until a meat thermometer inserted into the thickest part registers 150°F, about 40 minutes more.

Meanwhile, in a small bowl, whisk together the mustard, maple syrup, rosemary, lemon zest, and orange zest.

Brush the mustard mixture over the pork and return the pork to the oven. Roast until the glaze sets, 15 to 20 minutes. Remove from the oven and let the pork rest for 30 minutes.

Slice and serve with the sauce.

Corn Cream Sauce

Makes about 4 cups

4 tablespoons (½ stick) unsalted butter

¼ cup minced shallots

1 red bell pepper, finely diced

3½ cups fresh corn kernels

½ cup heavy cream

Salt and pepper

In a medium saucepan, melt the butter over medium heat. Add the shallots and bell pepper. Cook, stirring often, until the shallots are translucent, about 5 minutes.

Add the corn, cream, and a pinch each of salt and black pepper. Bring to a simmer, reduce the heat to low, cover, and cook, stirring occasionally, until the corn is tender, about 10 minutes.

Transfer ¼ cup of the mixture to a blender or food processor and puree until smooth (be careful when blending hot mixtures). Return the puree to the saucepan and mix well. Taste and season with salt and black pepper. Serve immediately. Leftover sauce can be stored in the refrigerator for up to 4 days.

Bourbon Praline Candied Baked Ham

Nothing dresses up a Southern table like glazed ham paired with potato salad. It's the equivalent of wrapping my favorite candy and my favorite pie around the goodness of a big smoked ham. Heaven.

Makes 8 to 10 servings

1 (8- to 10-pound) whole fully cooked skin-on
   smoked ham
2 cups unsalted chicken stock
½ onion, coarsely chopped
2 large carrots, coarsely chopped
4 bay leaves
3 whole peeled garlic cloves
¾ cup white vinegar
Bourbon Praline Sauce (recipe follows)

Preheat the oven to 350°F.

Using a sharp knife, score the skin of the ham into a diamond crosshatch pattern. Place the ham in a roasting pan. Surround it with the stock, onion, carrots, bay leaves, garlic, and vinegar. Cover the pan with aluminum foil.

Bake for 1½ hours.

Increase the oven temperature to 375°F. Transfer the ham to another roasting pan or a half-sheet pan; reserve the stock and vegetables for another use. Coat the ham with the sauce.

Bake until the ham gets some color, about 20 minutes. Let rest for 30 minutes before slicing.

Transfer the ham to a cutting board and carve. Serve hot with the pan sauce.

Bourbon Praline Sauce

Makes about 3½ cups

1 (1-pound) box dark brown sugar

½ cup yellow mustard

½ teaspoon ground nutmeg

1 teaspoon ground cinnamon

3 tablespoons ketchup

3 tablespoons fresh lemon juice

1 teaspoon pure vanilla extract

1 cup pecan halves, toasted

¼ cup bourbon

In a large heavy-bottomed saucepan, combine the brown sugar, mustard, nutmeg, cinnamon, ketchup, lemon juice, vanilla, and pecans. Bring to a simmer over medium heat, stirring. Reduce the heat to low and cook, stirring occasionally, until thick, about 20 minutes.

Remove from the heat and let cool for 20 minutes. Stir in the bourbon. Use immediately or store in an airtight container in the refrigerator for up to 1 month. Reheat before using, if chilled.

Prime Rib Roast
with Crawfish Onion Gravy

This is a dish for special guests and special occasions. This is an Uncle Joe dish full of drama, taste, and a big impression. It is a meat lover's paradise.

There's a real surf-and-turf moment here as well. There is something deliciously elegant about serving prime beef as a roast, with a rich seafood sauce.

Chef's tip: I sometimes substitute the crawfish for lump crabmeat, which can be easier to source than crawfish.

Makes 8 to 10 servings

¼ teaspoon coarsely ground black pepper

3 tablespoons salt

2 tablespoons chopped fresh rosemary

2 tablespoons minced garlic

1 (5-pound) bone-in beef rib roast, fat trimmed to about ⅛-inch thickness

Crawfish Onion Gravy (recipe follows)

Preheat the oven to 375°F. Fit a shallow roasting pan with a rack.

In a small bowl, combine the pepper, salt, rosemary, and garlic. Rub evenly over the rib roast. Place the roast, fat-side up, on the rack.

Roast until a meat thermometer inserted into the thickest part of the beef registers 130°F for medium-rare or 150°F for medium, 1 to 1½ hours. Let rest, tented with aluminum foil, for 20 minutes before carving.

Serve with the gravy.

Crawfish Onion Gravy

Makes about 1½ cups

8 tablespoons (1 stick) unsalted butter

1 large onion, finely chopped

1 red bell pepper, finely chopped

1 tablespoon rubbed sage

1½ tablespoons all-purpose flour

¼ cup chopped green onions

¼ cup heavy cream

1 cup unsalted chicken stock

⅛ teaspoon cayenne pepper

Salt and pepper

2 pounds shelled crawfish tail meat, chopped

In a large skillet, melt the butter over medium-high heat. Add the onion, bell pepper, and sage. Cook, stirring often, until the onion is translucent, about 3 minutes. Add the flour and green onions and cook, stirring, until well blended, 3 to 4 minutes.

Stir in the cream, stock, cayenne, and a pinch each of salt and black pepper. Cook, stirring, until thickened, about 5 minutes. Fold in the crawfish and cook until heated through, about 5 minutes. Serve immediately. Leftover sauce can be stored in the refrigerator for up to 4 days.

Braised Oxtails, Turnips, and Okra

The root
vegetables
give heft to
a dish where
the meat is
mostly for
flavoring.

Oxtails come out of the tradition of slaves making dinner from the scraps of the master's table. I did not grow up eating oxtails. I thought, *That's a lot of work for so little meat.* So when my mother prepared this dish, I would simply fill my plate with the amazing flavorful gravy, then grab a few of Mom's buttermilk biscuits and call it a day.

Moving to New York City exposed me to the extreme variety of ethnic foods available there. I discovered in the mom-and-pop storefront restaurants of the Caribbean community that there was a lot more to be enjoyed than the meat patties and jerk chicken I usually ordered. Once I started my restaurant career, I met so many different chefs, from Brazil to Jamaica, Trinidad to the Bahamas, Africa to Alabama. One of the dishes the chefs loved most and shared most often was oxtails, and they were so good.

While I was traveling in Bahia, Brazil, a friend's housekeeper made my uncle Joe's oxtail recipe with brown gravy and garnished it with my beloved okra. Imagine a family tradition being cooked by a little Brazilian woman so very far from my Carolina. After that, I was hooked. I only had to go halfway around the world to discover my family recipe, a variation of which you'll see here. I've added the turnips, which for me are a nice twist. The root vegetables give heft to a dish where the meat is mostly for flavoring.

Makes 6 servings

¼ cup vegetable oil

1 cup all-purpose flour

12 large oxtails

Salt and pepper

1½ (750-milliliter) bottles dry red wine

6 garlic cloves, smashed

1 large onion, coarsely chopped

2 celery stalks, chopped

1 large red bell pepper, coarsely chopped

1 teaspoon fresh thyme

1 teaspoon rubbed sage

1 teaspoon Old Bay seasoning

1 teaspoon celery flakes or seeds

2 bay leaves

2 cups canned diced tomatoes

4 medium turnips, peeled and cut into wedges

1 pound okra, trimmed and sliced

4 cups unsalted beef stock

Preheat the oven to 325°F.

In a large skillet, heat the oil over high heat.

Put the flour in a large bowl. Generously season the oxtails with salt and black pepper. Dredge the oxtails in the flour, shaking off any excess. Working in batches to avoid crowding the skillet, add the oxtails to the hot oil and cook, turning occasionally, until golden brown and crusty on all sides, about 2 minutes per side. Transfer to a deep, heavy roasting pan or Dutch oven in a single layer.

Meanwhile, in a large saucepan, bring the wine to a boil. Boil until reduced by half, about 20 to 30 minutes over medium-high heat. Add the wine to the roasting pan, then add the garlic, onion, celery, bell pepper, thyme, sage, Old Bay, celery flakes, bay leaves, and diced tomatoes. Cover with aluminum foil and transfer to the oven.

Bake until the oxtails are tender but the meat is not yet falling off the bone, about 3½ hours. Remove the pan from the oven but keep the oven on.

Using a slotted spoon, transfer the oxtails to a large bowl. Strain the braising liquid through a fine-mesh sieve and discard the solids. Return the liquid to the roasting pan and add the turnips, okra, and stock. Place the oxtails on top and return to the oven.

Roast until the turnips and okra are cooked through, about 20 minutes. Taste and season with salt and black pepper.

Arrange the oxtails on a large platter and serve.

6

Bread,
Biscuits,
and Muffins

Jukebox Music

Music is not math. It's science. You keep mixing the stuff up until it blows up on you, or it becomes this incredible potion.
—*Bruno Mars*

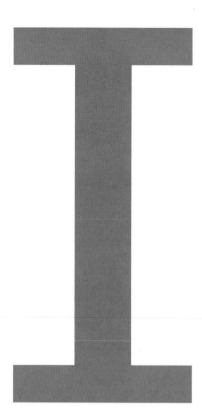I grew up during a time when the jukebox was filled with the best rhythm and blues: Wilson Pickett, Little Richard, James Brown, Sam Cooke, Otis Redding, and Fats Domino. Not to mention Ike and Tina Turner, Etta James, Chubby Checker, The Drifters, and The Platters.

Bankrolled by my grandpa, my uncle Joe (who was the chef) and my dad (who was Mr. Charm) owned and operated the Hilltop House, which was the hottest music review and club in town. My friends and I often got the job of cleaning the club on weekends. My dad would lock us in and put the jukebox on endless play. We would clean and dance and pretend we were performing all those songs: brooms and mop handles became microphones and dinner napkins became do-rags, those old-school head scarves that would transform Afros into slick waves.

It's been said that bars and broken hearts go hand in hand; if so, the jukebox was the ultimate matchmaker. You weren't tied down to the set list of a live band. Nor were you the passive recipient of the radio DJ's picks and preferences. The jukebox let you pick the song that perfectly suited your mood. There was never any shortage of songs to choose from. Just as a great supermarket can lure you in with something tempting on every aisle, a jukebox was grand enough to hold both who you were (the oldies), who you are (the top of the pops), and who you might someday be (the breaking tracks.)

A well-stocked kitchen is like a great jukebox: organized in a way that allows you to turn out your top ten favorites or new hits that drive friends and family wild. The jukebox's popularity was predicated on the idea that you put something simple in, like a coin, and something magical—a song—came out. Anyone who's ever baked knows that alchemy well. You start with ingredients that are by themselves nothing—a cup of flour, a quarter teaspoon of baking powder, a little milk, a half stick of butter—and you end up with a biscuit or a muffin or an angel roll, something that looks, feels, and tastes like a little bit of heaven.

When I opened my first restaurant, Café Beulah, I started creating flavored biscuits based on iconic Southern ingredients and jams and the proteins I would use to make biscuit sandwiches and sliders as a child. Café Beulah offered a breadbasket for purchase, which was rare in the early nineties. People weren't used to paying for bread, and I got a lot of pushback from some customers—until they ordered the basket, full of assorted biscuits and a variety of corn breads. Then they gladly saw the value. When I opened Shoebox Café, my restaurant in New York's Grand Central Terminal, we were known for the chubby biscuit: an oversized muffin type biscuit stuffed full of a variety of meats and jams, awesome Southern biscuits the likes of which you've always imagined. Biscuit heaven.

As with a great jukebox jam, to make a great biscuit, you must be willing to be

It's been said that bars and broken hearts go hand in hand; if so, the jukebox was the ultimate matchmaker.

generous with the good stuff. All flours are not alike, yet all will work. My choice is White Lily flour, as it is made to make the best possible biscuits. Go to town with your fillings, and try not to overcook your bread!

Buttermilk Corn Bread Muffins

This is a hearty bread that works with serious proteins: red meat, chicken, duck, and venison. It makes an equally great pairing with vegetables, hot or cold.

Makes 12

Nonstick cooking spray with flour (optional)
½ cup coarse white cornmeal
½ cup all-purpose flour
3 tablespoons light brown sugar
1½ teaspoons ground coriander
1 teaspoon baking powder
¼ teaspoon salt
¼ cup whole milk
¼ cup buttermilk
2 tablespoons vegetable oil
2 large eggs
¾ cup fresh corn kernels

Preheat the oven to 400°F. Line a 12-cup muffin pan with paper liners or coat the muffin cups with nonstick spray.

In a large bowl, whisk together the cornmeal, flour, brown sugar, coriander, baking powder, and salt. Whisk in the milk, buttermilk, and oil, then whisk in the eggs until the batter is smooth. Stir in the corn until well combined. Spoon the batter into the prepared muffin cups, dividing it evenly.

Bake until a toothpick inserted into the center of a muffin comes out clean, about 20 minutes. Serve immediately.

Buttermilk Biscuits

My mother and everybody else I knew made buttermilk biscuits: plain old delicious buttermilk biscuits.

My mother and everybody else I knew made buttermilk biscuits: plain old delicious buttermilk biscuits. Now and then there would be cheese biscuits at catered parties, smaller in size but full of cheese flavor. As a kid, I loved helping Mother mix and roll the dough, then take the biscuit cutter or a clean Mason jar to cut out circles of dough and place them on the cookie sheet or sheet pan to bake. One of the things I learned about biscuits was the amount of butter or shortening used could influence the flakiness of the biscuit.

Makes about 12

2 cups all-purpose flour, plus more for dusting

2½ teaspoons baking powder

¼ teaspoon baking soda

1 tablespoon sugar

1 teaspoon salt

4 tablespoons (½ stick) unsalted butter, cubed and chilled

¼ cup margarine or vegetable shortening, chilled

¾ cup buttermilk, chilled

In the bowl of a stand mixer, whisk together the flour, baking powder, baking soda, sugar, and salt by hand. Add the chilled butter, margarine, and buttermilk and, using the paddle attachment, beat the mixture on medium speed for no more than 12 seconds. Don't overblend or overwork the dough. You should still see pieces of the butter and margarine.

Scrape the dough onto a lightly floured board and form it into a ball. Dust with additional flour if the dough sticks to the board or your hands. Using a lightly floured rolling pin, roll out the dough to ½-inch thickness in a rectangular or round shape. Fold the dough in half, then repeat the rolling and folding twice more. Roll the dough out to ½-inch thick a final time, then, using a lightly floured 2½-inch biscuit cutter, cut out rounds of the dough, as close together as possible. Place the rounds, touching, on an ungreased half-sheet pan. Form the scraps into a ball and transfer them to the pan. (That becomes the "hoecake" you enjoy yourself.) Cover with plastic wrap and refrigerate for 1 to 2 hours or up to overnight. (The dough can be cut into biscuits and stored in airtight freezer wrap or containers in the freezer for up to 6 weeks, making doubling the recipe a good idea.)

When ready to bake the biscuits, preheat the oven 375°F.

Bake the biscuits until the tops are brown, 15 to 20 minutes. Serve immediately. Leftovers make great biscuit toast in the morning or snacks with your favorite toppings.

Sweet Potato Biscuits

This recipe marries the amazing depth of flavor in sweet potatoes with the crusty texture and delight of dough hot from the stove. When Mother pulled a tray of these flaky aromatic treasures from the oven, we were born again. Sweet potato biscuits were fancy, not for every day. These were for Sundays and holidays, special occasions when you put the best of your recipes on display.

Makes about 12

1 cup grated, blanched, and drained sweet potatoes

2 cups all-purpose flour, plus more for dusting

2½ teaspoons baking powder

¼ teaspoon baking soda

1 tablespoon sugar

1 teaspoon salt

4 tablespoons (½ stick) unsalted butter, cubed and chilled

¼ cup margarine or vegetable shortening, chilled

¾ cup buttermilk, chilled

In the bowl of a stand mixer, whisk together the flour, baking powder, baking soda, sugar, and salt by hand. Add the chilled butter, margarine, buttermilk, and grated sweet potatoes and, using the paddle attachment, beat the mixture on medium speed for no more than 12 seconds. Don't overblend or overwork the dough. You should still see pieces of the butter and margarine.

Scrape the dough onto a lightly floured board and form it into a ball. Dust with additional flour if the dough sticks to the board or your hands. Using a lightly floured rolling pin, roll out the dough to ½-inch thickness in a rectangular or round shape. Fold the dough in half, then repeat the rolling and folding twice more. Roll the dough out to ½-inch thick a final time, then, using a lightly floured 2½-inch biscuit cutter, cut out rounds of the dough, as close together as possible. Place the rounds, touching, on an ungreased half-sheet pan. Form the scraps into a ball and transfer them to the pan. (That becomes the "hoecake" you enjoy yourself.) Cover with plastic wrap and refrigerate for 1 to 2 hours or up to overnight.

When ready to bake the biscuits, preheat the oven 375°F.

Bake the biscuits until the tops are brown, 15 to 20 minutes. Serve immediately.

Jam Biscuits

Jam, jelly, and preserves were created for a biscuit, fresh out of the oven or a day old, split down the middle and toasted. My favorite way to pair them is to stuff the biscuits individually with jam before placing them in the oven to bake.

Chef's tip: You can also stuff these biscuits with squares of dark chocolate, crunchy peanut butter, cranberry relish, or berry compote.

Makes about 12

2 cups all-purpose flour, plus more for dusting

2½ teaspoons baking powder

¼ teaspoon baking soda

1 tablespoon sugar

1 teaspoon salt

4 tablespoons (½ stick) unsalted butter, cubed and chilled

¼ cup margarine or vegetable shortening, chilled

¾ cup buttermilk, chilled

Your favorite jam (½ teaspoon per biscuit)

In the bowl of a stand mixer, whisk together the flour, baking powder, baking soda, sugar, and salt by hand. Add the chilled butter, margarine, and buttermilk and, using the paddle attachment, beat the mixture on medium speed for no more than 12 seconds. Don't overblend or overwork the dough. You should still see pieces of the butter and margarine.

Scrape the dough onto a lightly floured board and form it into a ball. Dust with additional flour if the dough sticks to the board or your hands. Using a lightly floured rolling pin, roll out the dough to ½-inch thickness in a rectangular or round shape. Fold the dough in half, then repeat the rolling and folding twice more. Roll the dough out to ½-inch thick a final time, then, using a lightly floured 2½-inch biscuit cutter, cut out rounds of the dough, as close together as possible. Place the rounds, touching, on an ungreased half-sheet pan. Form the scraps into a ball and transfer them to the pan. (That becomes the "hoecake" you enjoy yourself.)

Using your thumb, make an indentation in the center of each biscuit and fill each indentation with ½ teaspoon of the jam. Cover with plastic wrap and chill for 1 to 2 hours or up to overnight.

When ready to bake the biscuits, preheat the oven 375°F.

Bake the biscuits until the tops are brown, 15 to 20 minutes. Serve immediately.

Jam, jelly, and preserves were created for a biscuit, fresh out of the oven or a day old, split down the middle and toasted.

Sage Sausage Biscuits

Sausage and biscuits are a hallmark south of the Mason-Dixon line. Better than an alarm clock and the beat of my mom's bedroom shoes against the hard oak floors in our Carolina home, the smell of sage sausage would wake me like clockwork every weekday morning. I created this recipe when I opened the Shoebox Café, my restaurant in New York's Grand Central Terminal. I wanted to give my customers at this busy train station a taste of my Southern memory, to go. Even now, I think of these biscuits as slow food for fast times: easy to make, easy to take, easy to savor en route or at your destination. Hopefully, you will enjoy them as much as I do.

Makes about 12

2 cups all-purpose flour, plus more for dusting

2½ teaspoons baking powder

¼ teaspoon baking soda

1 tablespoon sugar

1 teaspoon salt

4 tablespoons (½ stick) unsalted butter, cubed and chilled

¼ cup margarine or vegetable shortening, chilled

¾ cup buttermilk, chilled

1½ cups crumbled cooked sage sausage

In the bowl of a stand mixer, whisk together the flour, baking powder, baking soda, sugar, and salt by hand. Add the chilled butter, margarine, buttermilk, and crumbled sage sausage and, using the paddle attachment, beat the mixture on medium speed for no more than 12 seconds. Don't overblend or overwork the dough. You should still see pieces of the butter and margarine.

Scrape the dough onto a lightly floured board and form it into a ball. Dust with additional flour if the dough sticks to the board or your hands. Using a lightly floured rolling pin, roll out the dough to ½-inch thickness in a rectangular or round shape. Fold the dough in half, then repeat the rolling and folding twice more. Roll the dough out to ½-inch thick a final time, then, using a lightly floured 2½-inch biscuit cutter, cut out rounds of the dough, as close together as possible. Place the rounds, touching, on an ungreased half-sheet pan. Form the scraps into a ball and transfer them to the pan. (That becomes the "hoecake" you enjoy yourself.) Cover with plastic wrap and refrigerate for 1 to 2 hours or up to overnight.

When ready to bake the biscuits, preheat the oven 375°F.

Bake the biscuits until the tops are brown, 15 to 20 minutes. Serve immediately.

Jalapeño Cheddar Biscuits

Here I wanted to do something uniquely American and give a nod to Southwestern sensibilities: adding the heat of minced jalapeño gives just the right touch to the cheddar cheese.

Makes about 12

2 cups all-purpose flour, plus more for dusting

2½ teaspoons baking powder

¼ teaspoon baking soda

1 tablespoon sugar

1 teaspoon salt

3 tablespoons minced jalapeño

1 cup shredded sharp cheddar cheese

4 tablespoons (½ stick) unsalted butter, cubed and chilled

¼ cup margarine or vegetable shortening, chilled

¾ cup buttermilk, chilled

In the bowl of a stand mixer, whisk together the flour, baking powder, baking soda, sugar, and salt by hand. Stir in the jalapeños and cheese. Add the chilled butter, margarine, and buttermilk and, using the paddle attachment, beat the mixture on medium speed for no more than 12 seconds. Don't overblend or overwork the dough. You should still see pieces of the butter and margarine.

Scrape the dough onto a lightly floured board and form it into a ball. Dust with additional flour if the dough sticks to the board or your hands. Using a lightly floured rolling pin, roll out the dough to ½-inch thickness in a rectangular or round shape. Fold the dough in half, then repeat the rolling and folding twice more. Roll the dough out to ½-inch thick a final time, then, using a lightly floured 2½-inch biscuit cutter, cut out rounds of the dough, as close together as possible. Place the rounds, touching, on an ungreased half-sheet pan. Form the scraps into a ball and transfer them to the pan. (That becomes the "hoecake" you enjoy yourself.) Cover with plastic wrap and refrigerate for 1 to 2 hours or up to overnight. (The dough can be cut into biscuits and stored in the freezer for up to 6 weeks, making doubling the recipe a good idea.)

When ready to bake the biscuits, preheat the oven 375°F.

Bake the biscuits until the tops are brown, 15 to 20 minutes. Serve immediately. Leftovers make great biscuit toast in the morning or snacks with your favorite toppings.

Sweet Potato Muffins

In the South, we live for the flavor and satisfying taste of this amazing root vegetable. Now we find out it's nutritious, and we love it even more. You can play with this recipe as it handles spice well. Here I call for a bit of cinnamon and a kiss of nutmeg, but you could also try a dash of cayenne if you want it even spicier. The only thing missing is your favorite jam.

Makes 12

Nonstick cooking spray with flour (optional)

12 tablespoons (1½ sticks) unsalted butter, softened

¼ cup granulated sugar

¼ cup firmly packed dark brown sugar

2 large eggs

¾ cup mashed sweet potatoes

¼ cup buttermilk

¾ cup whole wheat flour

¾ cup all-purpose flour

1 teaspoon baking soda

1 teaspoon baking powder

½ teaspoon ground cinnamon

½ teaspoon ground nutmeg

½ teaspoon pure vanilla extract

¼ teaspoon salt

Preheat the oven to 400°F. Line a 12-cup muffin pan with paper liners or coat the muffin cups with nonstick spray.

In the bowl of a stand mixer fitted with the paddle attachment, beat the butter, granulated sugar, and brown sugar on medium-low speed until light and fluffy, 4 to 5 minutes. Add the eggs, one at a time, beating after each addition before adding the next.

Add the sweet potatoes, buttermilk, whole wheat flour, all-purpose flour, baking soda, baking powder, cinnamon, nutmeg, vanilla, and salt. Beat on low speed until everything is well mixed. Spoon the batter into the prepared muffin cups, dividing it evenly.

Bake until a toothpick inserted into the center of a muffin comes out clean, 18 to 20 minutes. Serve immediately.

If I could,
I would
bottle the
scent of
these rolls
rising in the
oven.

Angel Yeast Rolls

If I could, I would bottle the scent of
these rolls rising in the oven. As a kid, I
would drown a plateful of these in butter
and cane syrup and devour them before
I made it to the dinner table. As an adult,
I recognize that the treat of these is their
fluffy lightness and sweet bready flavor,
nothing else required!

Makes about 12

½ (¼-ounce) package active dry yeast (about
    1¼ teaspoons)
2 tablespoons warm water
2½ cups all-purpose flour, plus more for dusting
2 tablespoons sugar
1 teaspoon baking powder
½ teaspoon baking soda
⅛ teaspoon salt
½ cup vegetable shortening
1 cup buttermilk
4 tablespoons (½ stick) unsalted butter, melted
    and cooled

In a medium bowl, dissolve the yeast in
the warm water. Let stand until foamy,
about 5 minutes.

In a large bowl, whisk together the
flour, sugar, baking powder, baking soda,
and salt. Using a pastry blender, cut the
shortening into the flour mixture until the
mixture has the texture of coarse meal.

Add the buttermilk to the yeast mixture,
then add the buttermilk mixture to the
flour mixture and mix by hand to form a
soft dough.

Scrape the dough onto a lightly floured
board and knead until it comes together,
about 8 minutes. Form the dough into a
ball and let rest for 40 to 50 minutes.

Divide the dough into 12 pieces and
shape each into a ball. Place them on an
ungreased half-sheet pan, spacing them
a few inches apart. Cover lightly with a
clean kitchen towel and let rise in a warm,
draft-free area until doubled in size, 30 to
40 minutes.

Preheat the oven to 375°F.

Brush the risen dough balls with half
the melted butter. Bake until golden
brown, 15 to 20 minutes.

Brush with the remaining melted
butter and serve immediately.

Note

You can also
use a stand
mixer for this
recipe and
knead with a
dough hook
instead of by
hand.

7.

Cakes, Pies, and Puddings

Serenades

ck Out Receipt

lawn Branch
-887-1336
bcpl.info

rday, June 19, 2021 4:31:24 PM
1

: 31183200462403
e: Meals, music, and muses : recipes from my
ican American kitchen
no.: 641.5929 S
07/10/2021

l items: 1

just saved $35.00 by using your
ary today.

nded loan fees permanently
ended for all materials
ked out
youth library cards

When Nat King Cole sang songs like "Yes Sir, That's My Baby" and ballads like "Stardust," they weren't just love songs about a guy and a girl. His velvet-smooth voice somehow managed to convey that the love he sang about was big enough for any man, woman, or child who dared to open his or her heart. The very best serenades are generous: it's not singles versus couples, marrieds versus those who are in the throes of a full-blown one-sided crush. When a crooner like Cole takes hold of a song, there's enough love for all of us.

In our home, as in so many African American families, the preparation for Sunday supper began on Saturday night. Around eight in the evening, my mother and I would begin making the work-ahead dishes: pies, cakes, and angel yeast rolls. Sunday mornings were when the bulk of the meal prep would take place—the roasting, the frying, the boiling of potatoes and the bubbling pots of grits. Sunday morning was a mad dash—the goal was to have the bulk of the meal ready before Sunday service. But baking with my mother on Saturday night was a slow-paced luxury, as we chopped pecans, melted butter, beat eggs, and sifted flour in the cool of a Carolina evening, working quietly and purposefully from sunset until the stars shone bright.

The heritage of African American cuisine has something to offer everyone on the spectrum of sweetness, from the "so easy a child can make it" recipe for icebox lemon cake that was the pride of my elementary school cooking career to the practicality of a "store-bought piecrust won't kill you" recipe for blackberry cobbler to the "make 'em jealous, make 'em weak" triumph of a homemade coconut cake.

As Nat King Cole sang in "Sweet Lorraine," these are "just found joy/ happy as a baby boy" recipes. If you're an experienced baker, I think you'll enjoy this mix of Southern classics and playful riffs on old favorites.

New to baking? It requires focus and concentration, patience and resolve. Once you find your comfort and rhythm, you can take chances: be improvisational and

New to baking?
It requires focus
and concentration,
patience and
resolve. Once you
find your comfort
and rhythm, you
can take chances.

experimental. My advice to a beginner is
to follow the recipe to the letter. Baking
is based on a combination of measured
ingredients that come together to yield
a formulated result. As your comfort
develops, so will your ability to take
liberties.

Take heart. Nothing will endear you to
the people you cook for like a homemade
dessert. Be gentle with yourself as you
make your way through this section. You
must sing a song many times before it
becomes truly your own. With patience
and passion, these recipes can become
treasured tentpoles of your culinary
playlist. Serve any of these confections,
and your guests will declare, in the words
of Marvin Gaye's classic tune, "How sweet
it is to be loved by you."

Sticky Buns

Absolutely nobody made sticky buns like my grandma. In a round buttered tin pan, she could whip these buns up so fast and so often that it was simply expected and eagerly awaited. For breakfast or midday snack, a sticky bun was a panacea for everything that was wrong in a child's world. The only problem was stopping yourself from eating too many too quickly. Delicious. So when I was curating recipes I cherish and love for this book, sticky buns were top of mind.

My tip for you is again be adventurous with these. Once you get your technique right, the fun begins. Play with the flavor profile, try adding chocolate chips, candied ginger, even cocoa powder in the cinnamon-sugar mixture. I have also added crumbled bacon to my toppings. Just make the dish yours and have fun with it!

Makes 12

Dough

¼ cup warm water

1 (¼-ounce) package active dry yeast

¼ cup sugar

1 cup whole milk

4 tablespoons (½ stick) unsalted butter, softened, plus more for the bowl

3 large egg yolks

⅛ teaspoon salt

4 cups all-purpose flour, plus more as needed

Filling

½ cup firmly packed light brown sugar

1 tablespoon ground cinnamon

4 tablespoons (½ stick) unsalted butter, melted, plus more for brushing

Topping

1 cup firmly packed light brown sugar

4 tablespoons (½ stick) unsalted butter

1 tablespoon light corn syrup

1½ cups pecans, chopped

½ cup rum-soaked black currants

For the dough: In the bowl of a stand mixer fitted with the dough hook, mix the water, yeast, and sugar until the sugar has dissolved and let sit until foamy, about 5 minutes.

Add the milk, butter, egg yolks, salt, and 3 cups of the flour. Mix on low speed until blended. Add the remaining 1 cup flour. Increase the speed to medium and knead until the dough is smooth and sticky, 3 to 5 minutes. Add more flour, a tablespoon at a time, if the dough is too wet. It should be tight and spongy but not oozy.

Grease a large bowl with butter. Shape the dough into a ball and place it in the bowl. Turn the dough to coat with the butter. Cover with plastic wrap and let rise until doubled in size, about 1 hour.

Punch down the dough and turn it out onto a lightly floured surface. Let the dough sit, covered with a cloth, while you make the filling.

For the filling: In a small bowl, combine the brown sugar and cinnamon. Stir in the melted butter until evenly moistened.

Using a lightly floured rolling pin, roll the dough out into a ¼-inch-thick rectangle. Brush with additional melted butter and sprinkle evenly with the filling. Starting from one long side, tightly roll up the dough into a log, jelly roll–style. Set the log seam-side down and cut it crosswise into 12 slices.

For the topping: In a small saucepan, combine the brown sugar, butter, and corn syrup. Cook over low heat, stirring, until the butter has melted. Pour the mixture into a 9 x 13-inch cake pan and sprinkle evenly with the chopped pecans and drained rum-soaked currants.

Place the buns cut-side down in the pan on top of the pecan mixture, making sure the buns are touching. Cover and chill overnight.

When ready to bake the buns, preheat the oven to 375°F. Remove the buns from the refrigerator and let them come to room temperature, about an hour.

Bake the buns until golden, about 35 minutes. Remove from the oven and immediately invert the buns onto a large platter, being careful to not burn yourself with the hot topping. Serve immediately.

Doughnuts

I remember the first time I ate a doughnut. Mother, as she always did when serious cooking was about to take place, grabbed the cast-iron skillet, and to my amazement, she made something I'd never tasted before: doughnuts. I'm not saying that once you've had homemade, you'll never go back to store-bought doughnuts, but I will say that nothing out of a wrapper can compare with a doughnut fresh from the pan.

Makes 12

1 large egg
½ cup sugar
2 tablespoons vegetable shortening, melted
½ cup buttermilk
1 cup all-purpose flour, plus more for dusting
½ teaspoon ground nutmeg
2 teaspoons baking powder
¼ teaspoon baking soda
¼ teaspoon salt
Peanut, canola, or vegetable oil, for frying

In a large bowl, mix together the egg, sugar, melted shortening, and buttermilk. Add the flour, nutmeg, baking powder, baking soda, and salt. Mix well.

Turn the dough out onto a floured board. Using a floured rolling pin, roll the dough to ¼-inch thickness. Using a floured doughnut cutter, cut out 12 doughnuts. Gather the scraps, roll them out to ¼-inch thickness, and cut into strips.

Fill a large cast-iron skillet with oil to a depth of 1 inch. Heat over medium-high heat to 350°F. Working in batches to avoid crowding the skillet, add the doughnuts to the hot oil and fry, turning once, until golden brown, about 2 minutes per side. Drain on a crumpled brown paper bag or paper towels. Repeat to fry the dough strips.

Serve immediately.

All you
need to
know is
that this is
the easiest
pie you'll
ever make.

Icebox Lemon Pie

This is the first pie I ever made, and it quickly became the pie of my childhood and my dreams, an obsession that took years to get under control. It was a long time before I could find a way to be in the same room as a graham cracker crust filled with lemony goodness and not lose my mind.

All you need to know is that this is the easiest pie you'll ever make. You literally can't mess it up. It is the perfect dessert after a spicy or robust meal. It's also a great pie to have on hand when you're making something new and untested. No matter what the result of your culinary adventures, this dessert will save the moment and will be all anyone will talk about. That's a recipe worth committing to memory, don't you think?

Makes one 9-inch pie

(continued)

Crust

2½ cups graham cracker crumbs

12 tablespoons (1½ sticks) unsalted butter, melted

¼ cup sugar

Filling

3 large eggs, separated

Juice of 3 lemons

1 (14-ounce) can sweetened condensed milk

1 teaspoon cream of tartar

3 tablespoons sugar

For the crust: Preheat the oven to 300°F.

In a medium bowl, combine the graham cracker crumbs, melted butter, and sugar until the crumbs are evenly moistened. Press the mixture into the bottom and sides of a 9-inch pie tin.

For the filling: Cover and chill the egg whites. In a medium bowl, combine the egg yolks, lemon juice, and condensed milk. Mix well and pour over the graham cracker crust.

Bake until stiff, about 30 minutes. Let cool to room temperature, then chill for at least 3 hours or up to overnight.

When ready to assemble the pie, preheat the oven to 350°F.

In the bowl of a stand mixer fitted with the whisk attachment, beat the egg whites and cream of tartar on high speed. With the mixer running, gradually add the sugar and beat until stiff peaks form.

Spread the meringue over the pie filling.

Bake until the meringue is golden brown, about 12 minutes. Let cool for 30 minutes, then chill for 30 minutes before serving.

Bourbon Pecan Pie

Everything in life tastes better with bourbon . . . and pecan pie is no exception. The sweet, sticky, crunchy bite of one of the South's most delicate and indulgent desserts fares well with a splash of bourbon, that oaky aged elixir from Kentucky. Pecan pie was one of the first pies I learned to bake.

The recipe is pretty basic, but it's those special touches that will distinguish your pie, like the quality of the crust and whether you use dark, light, or golden syrup as your base. I like to make a couple of these pies at a time and freeze one to enjoy later with friends and family at a moment's notice. It defrosts well and quickly. Enjoy!

Makes one 9-inch pie

1 cup light or dark corn syrup

3 large eggs

1 cup sugar

2 tablespoons unsalted butter, melted

¼ teaspoon ground cinnamon

⅛ teaspoon ground nutmeg

½ teaspoon lemon zest

2 tablespoons bourbon

1 teaspoon pure vanilla extract

1½ cups pecans

1 Pie Shell (recipe follows), chilled

Preheat the oven to 350°F.

In a large bowl, whisk together the corn syrup, eggs, sugar, melted butter, cinnamon, nutmeg, lemon zest, bourbon, and vanilla. Stir in the pecans. Pour the mixture into the pie shell.

Bake on the center rack of the oven until an instant-read thermometer inserted into the center registers 200°F and the top springs back when tapped lightly, 55 to 60 minutes.

Let cool until warm and serve.

Pie Shell

Makes one 9-inch pie shell

1 cup all-purpose flour, plus more for dusting

½ teaspoon salt

2 tablespoons vegetable shortening, chilled

3 tablespoons unsalted butter, chilled

¼ cup ice water

In a food processor, pulse the flour, salt, shortening, and butter until the mixture resembles coarse meal. Drizzle the water through the feed tube and pulse until the dough comes together to form a ball. Shape the dough into a disc, wrap in plastic wrap, and chill for at least 1 hour or up to overnight.

On a lightly floured board using a lightly floured rolling pin, roll out the dough into a round larger than a 9-inch pie tin so there is some overhang. Transfer the dough to the pie tin and crimp the edges. Chill until firm before filling, 10 to 15 minutes.

Chess Pie

This pie is a bit of a mystery. In England, a lemon curd pie is called "cheese pie" and perhaps the Americanized version became "chess pie." Another strain of culinary lore suggests that this pie was what the menfolk were served before they retired to the game room to play cards or chess. Still others claim that it's a play on the Southern dialect: "jes' pie" (or "just pie") became "chess pie." I didn't grow up eating this pie, but as an adult who loves custards, I immediately gravitated toward it. Whether you call it "jes' pie" or "chess pie," I think you'll find it easy to make and even easier to love.

Makes one 9-inch pie

8 tablespoons (1 stick) unsalted butter, softened

1 cup granulated sugar

¼ cup firmly packed light brown sugar

4 large eggs

1½ cups buttermilk

2 tablespoons fine white cornmeal

3 tablespoons fresh lemon juice

1 teaspoon pure vanilla extract

⅛ teaspoon salt

1 Pie Shell (page 186), chilled

Preheat the oven to 350°F.

In a large bowl, cream together the butter and both sugars. Beat in the eggs, one at a time. Add the buttermilk, cornmeal, lemon juice, vanilla, and salt. Beat until well blended. Pour the mixture into the pie shell.

Bake until a knife inserted into the center of the pie comes out clean, 35 to 40 minutes.

Let cool until warm or at room temperature and serve.

Banana Pudding Custard Pie

Bananas are a relatively late addition to American cuisine. It wasn't until after the Civil War and the rise of the Industrial Age that steamships made importing the easily perishable fruit a reality. Rare and delicious, bananas soon became a premium ingredient, hence the always luxurious air that accompanies this pie.

Chef's tip: The secret to making custard pies is controlling the heat of the stove: it should be intense enough to advance the cooking process but not so hot that it scorches the custard.

Makes one 9-inch pie

Crust

1½ cups whole vanilla wafers

4 tablespoons (½ stick) unsalted butter, melted

2 tablespoons sugar

Filling

3 large eggs, separated

3 tablespoons cornstarch

1 cup whole milk

½ cup heavy cream

1 cup plus 3 tablespoons sugar

1 teaspoon unsalted butter, melted

1½ teaspoons pure vanilla extract

⅛ teaspoon salt

½ teaspoon cream of tartar

3 bananas, cut into ¼-inch-thick slices

1 cup whole vanilla wafers

For the crust: Preheat the oven to 325°F.

Place the vanilla wafers in a food processor and pulse until the crumbs resemble coarse meal. Add the melted butter and sugar and pulse until the cookie crumbs are evenly moistened. Press the mixture into the bottom and sides of a 9-inch pie tin.

Bake the crust until set and golden brown, about 10 minutes. Let cool completely.

For the filling: Cover and chill the egg whites. In a medium saucepan, combine the cornstarch, milk, cream, egg yolks, and 1 cup of the sugar. Cook over medium heat, whisking continuously, until thickened, 10 to 15 minutes. Do not leave the custard unattended while whisking because the egg yolks will cook and make the mixture grainy. Whisk in the butter, vanilla, and salt. Pour the custard into the baked crust and chill for at least 2 hours or up to overnight.

When ready to assemble the pie, preheat the oven to 375°F.

In the bowl of a stand mixer fitted with the whisk attachment, combine the egg whites and the cream of tartar. With the mixer on high speed, gradually add the remaining 3 tablespoons sugar and whisk until stiff peaks form.

Arrange the banana slices in a single layer over the custard. Top the banana slices with the vanilla wafers. Spread the meringue over the wafers, covering the entire pie.

Bake until the meringue is light brown all over, about 10 minutes. Let cool to room temperature, then chill for at least 20 minutes before serving.

Sweet Potato Pie

Once upon a time, the great Ray Charles sang a song about sweet potato pie. He described being on cloud nine for one reason alone: sweet potato pie.

There has never been a time in my life when sweet potato pie was not a welcome sight. The ground cloves may be a surprise ingredient for aficionados of this pie, but I love it.

Makes one 9-inch pie

2 pounds sweet potatoes

½ cup sweetened condensed milk

¾ cup heavy cream

4 large eggs

4 tablespoons (½ stick) unsalted butter, melted

1 cup sugar

1 teaspoon pure vanilla extract

½ teaspoon ground cinnamon

¼ teaspoon ground nutmeg

¼ teaspoon ground cloves

1 Pie Shell (page 186), chilled

Preheat the oven to 425°F.

Place the sweet potatoes on a half-sheet pan. Roast until soft, about 1 hour. You should be able to drive a fork into them when they're ready. Reduce the oven temperature to 350°F. Set the sweet potatoes aside until cool enough to handle.

Peel the sweet potatoes and place the flesh in a large bowl. Mash well, then add the condensed milk, cream, eggs, melted butter, sugar, vanilla, cinnamon, nutmeg, and cloves. Using a heavy whisk, whisk until smooth. Pour the mixture into the pie shell.

Bake until the filling is set, 40 to 50 minutes. Let cool to room temperature and serve.

Carolina Rice Pudding

I treat rice pudding like crème brûlée, a French pudding with Carolina roots. This is a heritage pudding, and the foundation of the recipe is how my family made it. The dried cherries are my own addition. At home, I would also whip up a bourbon syrup or add a scoop of rum raisin ice cream. A sprig of mint or some crumbled candied pralines would also make a wonderful topping. It is a Willy Wonka–like treat, the sweet base for anything your heart desires.

Makes 6 servings

1¼ cups Carolina long-grain rice

1½ cups whole milk

½ cup sugar

¼ teaspoon salt

½ cup heavy cream

½ cup golden raisins

½ cup dried cherries

¼ teaspoon ground nutmeg

¼ teaspoon ground cinnamon

½ teaspoon pure vanilla extract

1½ tablespoons unsalted butter

Rinse the rice with cold water until the water runs clear (this removes excess starch). Drain.

In a large saucepan, bring 1½ cups water to a boil over medium-high heat. Stir in the rice and return the water to a boil. Reduce the heat to low, cover, and cook until tender, about 20 minutes.

Add the milk, sugar, salt, cream, raisins, cherries, nutmeg, and cinnamon. Cook, stirring, until creamy, about 20 minutes.

Remove from the heat and stir in the vanilla and butter. Serve warm or cold.

Blackberry Cobbler

Goodness on a vine. You simply can't talk about the South without talking about blackberries as a characteristic ingredient of Southern living. I could never get enough of this berry as a child: in a cobbler, in a pie, on Sunday afternoon with freshly churned ice cream. My friends and I would set out with buckets and sticks to harvest gallons of these berries. We would set off on a mission with our hopes high and buckets empty. The motivation was that there was no shortage of households willing to buy the berries. But for me, the money I could earn was small tidings compared with what I knew Mother could create with a bucket full of berries. My goal was always to collect enough berries for two pies.

As these outings were usually on a Saturday afternoon, I knew those amazing pies were destined for the Sunday supper, my favorite meal of the week. Blackberry cobbler placed on the dining table with a tub of homemade ice cream was the closest I would get to

(continued)

You simply can't talk about the South without talking about blackberries.

Blackberry Cobbler (*continued*)

heaven on that day, whether I'd gone to church or not.

Makes 6 servings

4 cups fresh blackberries

1¼ cups sugar

½ teaspoon ground cinnamon

¼ teaspoon ground nutmeg

½ teaspoon finely minced fresh ginger

1 teaspoon pure vanilla extract

2 tablespoons fresh lemon juice

2 tablespoons cornstarch

3 tablespoons cold water

1 cup all-purpose flour

1¼ teaspoons baking powder

½ teaspoon salt

5 tablespoons cold unsalted butter

¼ cup buttermilk, chilled

Whipped cream or ice cream, for serving (optional)

Preheat the oven to 350°F.

In a medium saucepan, sprinkle the blackberries with ¼ cup of the sugar. Add the cinnamon, nutmeg, ginger, vanilla extract, lemon juice, cornstarch, and cold water and toss well to combine. Bring to a boil over medium-high heat. Immediately pour the blackberry mixture into a 9-inch deep-dish pie tin or a greased glass or ceramic pie dish.

In a large bowl, combine the remaining 1 cup sugar, the flour, baking powder, and salt. Using a pastry blender, cut in the butter until the mixture resembles coarse meal. While stirring, gradually add the buttermilk. Mix well to combine. Drop the dough by spoonfuls on top of the blackberries.

Bake until the dough is golden, 40 to 50 minutes.

Serve immediately with whipped cream or ice cream, if desired.

Southern Pound Cake

Don't let the simplicity of this cake fool you.

Pound cake got its name from its easy-to-remember basic recipe: a pound of this and a pound of that, basic and straightforward, like most Southerners. But don't let the simplicity of this cake fool you—many an ambitious cook has tried and failed to produce a pound cake with all the flavor and texture required to be the *best* pound cake.

Pound cakes were the type of cake people based their reputations on. Not everyone achieved bragging rights for this cake . . . but those who did were unquestionably revered. Ms. Means, who lived next door to my grandfather, was one of those people. It was known that she made one of the best pound cakes in town, and if you didn't know, you'd better ask somebody.

Most people overcook it or undercook it. A dry pound cake is not the worst thing in the world: you can slice it, butter it, top it with fruit, whipped cream, maybe some ice cream. It's also great sliced and toasted and used in a trifle with custard, cream, fruit, and a splash of your favorite spirits or brandy.

But the goal is to make an *amazing* pound cake, light and airy to the touch, moist and flavorful. I promise you, this recipe works.

Makes one 9-inch tube cake

1 cup (2 sticks) cold unsalted butter, plus more for the pan

2 cups cake flour, plus more for the pan

⅛ teaspoon salt

Zest of 1 lemon

1⅔ cups sugar

5 large eggs, at room temperature

¼ cup sour cream

¼ cup heavy cream

2 teaspoons pure vanilla extract

Preheat the oven to 350°F. Butter the bottom of a 9-inch tube pan and lightly dust it with flour, tapping out any excess.

In a medium bowl, combine the cake flour, salt, and lemon zest.

In the bowl of a stand mixer fitted with the paddle attachment, cream the butter and sugar on medium speed until smooth and fluffy. Add the eggs, one at a time, beating after each addition before adding the next. Beat until the mixture is light and fluffy. Add the sour cream, heavy cream, and vanilla and beat until smooth.

With the mixer on low speed, add the flour mixture in thirds, mixing well after each addition before adding the next. Pour the batter into the prepared pan; tap the pan against the counter to get rid of any air bubbles.

Bake until a knife inserted into the center of the cake comes out clean, 45 to 50 minutes.

Let cool in the pan for 15 minutes before inverting onto a serving platter. Let cool until warm and serve.

Southern Comfort Peach Shortcake

While Georgia is known as the peach state, peaches are the true fruit of South Carolina: we produce twice as many as our Georgia neighbors. From peach brandy to peach cobbler, we love our peaches any way we can get them. For me, nothing was better on a hot July day after a Sunday platter of fried chicken or smoked ham than a great peach cobbler with a scoop of vanilla ice cream.

This is my refreshing remix of that cobbler. Peach shortcake is a wonderful light mix of sweet fruity filling with whipped-to-perfection cream.

Chef's tip: One way to make this dessert special is to make individual serving–size cakes in small tins or a muffin pan. To make it even fancier, serve each mini shortcake on its own plate, garnished with micro mint and edible flowers.

Makes one 9-inch cake

Nonstick cooking spray

1½ cups all-purpose flour

½ cup plus 2½ tablespoons sugar

1 tablespoon baking powder

⅛ teaspoon salt

3 tablespoons vegetable shortening, chilled

2 tablespoons cold unsalted butter

¾ cup buttermilk, chilled

1 large egg, beaten

4 cups sliced fresh peaches

½ cup Southern Comfort

1 cup heavy cream, whipped

Preheat the oven to 425°F. Coat a 9-inch round cake pan with nonstick spray.

In a medium bowl, combine the flour, 2½ tablespoons of the sugar, the baking powder, and the salt. Using a pastry blender, cut in the shortening and butter until the mixture resembles coarse meal. Slowly fold in the buttermilk and beaten egg until well mixed. Spread the dough into the prepared pan.

Bake until golden brown, about 20 minutes. Turn the shortcake out onto a wire rack to cool slightly.

Meanwhile, in a large glass bowl, combine the peaches, the remaining ½ cup sugar, and the Southern Comfort. Let stand for 30 minutes.

Slice the shortcake in half horizontally. Spread half the peach mixture over the cut side of one cake half. Top with half the whipped cream and place the remaining cake half on top, cut-side down. Spread the remaining peach mixture on top of the cake and top with the remaining whipped cream. Slice and serve immediately.

For me, nothing was better on a hot July day after a Sunday platter of fried chicken or smoked ham than a great peach cobbler with a scoop of vanilla ice cream.

Chocolate Pineapple Upside-Down Cake

There is not an authentic Southern table in existence south of the Mason-Dixon line that has not hosted, on any given Sunday dinner, a pineapple upside-down cake.

I developed this recipe for Chocolate Pineapple Upside-Down Cake as a way to elevate the level of surprise and drama at the end of a fine American meal. Just when it wasn't supposed to get any better, this dessert ensures it does.

Makes one 9-inch cake

4 tablespoons (½ stick) unsalted butter

2 cups canned crushed pineapple

½ cup firmly packed dark brown sugar

1½ cups all-purpose flour

½ cup unsweetened cocoa powder

1½ teaspoons baking powder

¾ cup granulated sugar

1 teaspoon ground cinnamon

1 teaspoon ground ginger

2 teaspoons pure vanilla extract

2 large eggs

½ cup whole milk

½ cup vegetable oil

1 cup bittersweet chocolate chips

Preheat the oven to 350°F.

Place the butter in a 9-inch round cake pan with 2-inch sides. Set the pan in the oven until the butter is melted, 4 to 5 minutes. Remove from the oven, but keep the oven on.

Sprinkle the crushed pineapple on top of the melted butter. Top with the brown sugar. Set aside.

In the bowl of a stand mixer fitted with the whisk attachment, combine the flour, cocoa powder, baking powder, granulated sugar, cinnamon, and ginger. Whisk at low speed until well combined. Add the vanilla, eggs, milk, oil, and chocolate chips. Increase the speed to medium and whisk until smooth. Pour the batter into the pan over the brown sugar and pineapple.

Bake until a knife inserted into the center of the cake comes out clean, 45 to 50 minutes.

Let the cake cool in the pan for 20 minutes. Run a knife around the sides of the pan to loosen the cake. Place a serving platter over the pan and, holding the platter and pan together, invert the cake onto the platter. Tap the bottom of the pan lightly to release the pineapple topping and remove the pan.

Let cool until warm and serve.

Sweet Potato Coconut Cake

This is one of my top three favorite cakes. Coconut cake is the most regal, dramatic, and elegant of Southern cakes. I could absolutely not write this cookbook without featuring a coconut cake. I wanted to give you a contemporary cake full of the flavors and traditional notes of the South: the coconut, the yam or sweet potato, rich sour cream, and aromatic notes of cinnamon, nutmeg, and the surprise of ginger, all balanced with the best vanilla you can buy.

Makes one 10-inch Bundt cake

Nonstick cooking spray (optional)

2½ cups all-purpose flour, plus more for the pan

1½ teaspoons baking powder

1 teaspoon ground cinnamon

½ teaspoon ground nutmeg

½ teaspoon ground ginger

⅛ teaspoon salt

8 tablespoons (1 stick) unsalted butter, softened

1 cup granulated sugar

3 large eggs

1½ cups grated peeled sweet potatoes

1 cup finely grated fresh or unsweetened shredded coconut

½ cup sour cream

1 teaspoon pure vanilla extract

1 cup whole milk

Confectioners' sugar, for dusting

Whipped cream, for serving

Preheat the oven to 350°F. Coat the bottom of a 10-inch Bundt pan with cooking spray or butter and lightly dust it with flour, tapping out any excess.

In a medium bowl, combine the flour, baking powder, cinnamon, nutmeg, ginger, and salt. Set aside.

In the bowl of a stand mixer fitted with the paddle attachment, cream the butter and granulated sugar on medium speed until smooth and fluffy. Add the eggs, one at a time, beating after each addition before adding the next. Beat until the mixture is light and fluffy. Add the grated sweet potatoes, coconut, sour cream, and vanilla and beat until smooth.

With the mixer on low speed, add the flour mixture in thirds, alternating with the milk and ending with the dry ingredients. Beat on low speed until well incorporated. Pour the batter into the prepared pan.

Bake until a knife inserted into the center of the cake comes out clean, 40 to 45 minutes.

Let cool in the pan for 15 minutes. Place a serving plate over the pan and invert the cake onto the plate. Let cool until warm before slicing.

Slice and dust with confectioners' sugar. Serve topped with whipped cream.

Bourbon Chocolate Praline Truffles

After a night at the theater or musical concert, I like to plan a light late supper for friends. One I cook ahead and simply serve in less than thirty minutes . . . easy and understated. Being a late night, the truffles are the perfect option with after-dinner drinks. We often find ourselves at the piano in full song and merriment; the truffles are better than a heavy dessert so you can indulge and still sing your heart out.

These Bourbon Chocolate Praline Truffles are really a Southern explosion in a ball of flavor. I love serving this sweet dish. It can be made days in advance and brought to room temperature while the entrée is served. When entertaining at my house, I overcook purposely so most everyone leaves with a to-go bag of these sweet treats.

Chef's tip: Keeping the temperature of the chocolate mixture cool is the key to shaping and molding the candies.

Makes about 55 truffles

(continued)

Bourbon Chocolate Praline Truffles (*continued*)

Truffles

8 ounces semisweet chocolate, chopped

8 ounces bittersweet chocolate, chopped

1 cup heavy cream

½ cup finely chopped toasted pecans

2 tablespoons bourbon

Pralines

¾ cup firmly packed light brown sugar

¾ cup heavy cream

4 tablespoons (½ stick) unsalted butter

2 teaspoons pure vanilla extract

1 cup chopped pecans

For the truffles: In the top of a double boiler or in a heatproof bowl set over a saucepan of simmering water, combine both chocolates, the cream, pecans, and bourbon and heat over medium-low heat, stirring often, until melted and smooth. Remove from the heat and let cool to room temperature, then chill until the chocolate mixture is firm enough to roll.

Using a melon baller, scoop the chocolate mixture and then roll into balls. Set aside on a baking sheet or cutting board.

For the pralines: In a medium saucepan, combine the brown sugar and cream and heat over medium-low heat, stirring, until the brown sugar has melted. Cook, stirring occasionally, until blended into a paste, about 10 minutes. Add the butter, vanilla, and pecans. Cook, stirring, for 5 minutes.

Line a half-sheet pan with parchment paper. Drop the pralines by tablespoons onto the prepared pan and let cool completely. When cool, chop until almost the texture of a fine dust and place in a medium bowl.

Working in batches, drop the truffles into the bowl and toss to coat. Place them on the parchment-lined pan as you go. Serve immediately or store in an airtight container in the refrigerator for up to 5 days or in the freezer for up to 1 month.

After a night at the theater or musical concert, I like to plan a light late supper for friends.

Acknowledgments

This book celebrates the foodways of the ancestors, extraordinary people who gave the ultimate price for being Black in a hostile, unaccepting world. Families and communities of doers and achievers, despite enslaved conditions, were the cultural foundation of agriculture and culinary tradition in America, as planters, farmers, and domestics, raising this country's wealth one seed at a time. Hardworking people who gave all they had and more, not knowing their lives would create a lasting legacy. Tracing the steps of our ancestral people, we fuse together a culinary conversation in the kitchen. We pay homage to the crossroads of their lives through food and culture, bringing attention and reverence to their influence on global cuisine. Hopefully, and humbly, paying tribute to years of unsung people who gave so much of themselves and received so little in return, we celebrate the ancestors and appreciate all they gifted us. In so doing, I also want to thank the many partners, collaborators, supporters, and special people who helped me realize every aspect of this journey: the recipes for food and life, this manuscript we serve, this cookbook we've created.

To my family, especially my parents, Johnnie Mae and Alex Smalls, who loved me deeply. My grandpa Ed Smalls, who taught me the power and meaning of gardening and the difference between fresh, local, organic foods and supermarket items. Thank you to Uncle Joe and Aunt Laura, who taught me that my dreams mattered and would guide me through life. To my sisters, Cynthia, Delores, and Elonda, who hold me now that the previous generation has taken flight. I appreciate you and I love you. It's our time to buttress the next generation, to give them our best, so they grow to be their best selves. And my thanks to a host of relatives who cooked and farmed, sharing the lessons of their trades, trials, and struggles, their strength and determination, with me.

A huge thank-you to Veronica Chambers for her brilliant literary architectural skills, intuitive expressions, and stylistic contributions to this book.

Her discipline to scholarship and task was always present. Her commitment to excellence that never wavered got it done. She really helped me tell my story. Veronica, you're an important ingredient in this recipe.

A huge debt of gratitude and appreciation to Victoria Sanders, not only my literary agent and dear friend for more than years do us justice but I can also honestly say we are family. For more than forty years she has fed my story and held my hand in various ways, making sure I got from one side of the river to the other. I couldn't have navigated this life as well as I have without her. She is my rock and my warrior. . . . Believe it! Thanks to her great team of professionals who understand what the job really is and get it done. Special shout-out to Bernadette, too.

A big thanks to Will Schwalbe of Flatiron Books and his commitment to making this book everything we dreamed it should be. To his team of smart folks who go the distance and get things done. Our second book together! With appreciation to Beatriz Da Costa,

who captured the photogenic vision of our mission with brilliance and heart. Every dish leaps off the page—love your work! And to Roscoe Betsill, your stylistic approach to food on a plate made all the difference in every shot. A big thank-you—you have taught me what a really good food stylist is all about! And we all know the importance of a recipe, but no one knows this better than Genevieve Ko. Thank you for bringing such positive energy and expertise to the writing

and organization of every recipe. Your expertise ensures that everyone will make the same dish we intended every time. I hope we work together again soon.

And to Margaret Braun and Luz Ceramics—thank you for lending us your beautiful pieces. I want to give a special shout-out to all my great friends who made time to test out one recipe after another. You are the best. So glad I decided to share the task with all of you. My culinary village helpers, we did it! Thank you to that very close group of friends— you know who you are—who command and own a seat at my table and who

are a significant part of the Alexander experience, part of my love fest, cut from the same cloth and fabric of our lives. I love you more than you know.

To all the Black chefs, young and old, working in the hospitality world, creating the foods of their ancestors—heritage cooking made with pride and dignity, love and reverence—this book is for you. I am proud to be one of you, cooking the foods of our ancestral trust. Keeping the foodways of our forefathers alive and our culture intact for future generations.

And last, to the Harlem community, where I live and belong. Thank you, Harlem, for being the brilliant multicultural oasis that you are, a community that speaks to my heart, soul, and spirit. You give me life and the perfect cradle to exist in. Thanks for the support and encouraging me to dream. You make it real: this place we love between Harlem and heaven.

Appendix
Chapter Playlists

Here is music to go with each chapter—for you to play while cooking, eating, or just reading to recipes. I hope these selections inspire you as they have me. These are just a few of my favorites, and I'm sure you will want to discover your own.

1. Jazz

"Here's to Life" by Shirley Horn

"See-line Woman" by Nina Simone

"What a Wonderful World" by Louis Armstrong

"Come Sunday" by Dee Dee Bridgewater

"Take the 'A' Train" by Duke Ellington and Ella Fitzgerald

"Lush Life" by John Coltrane and Johnny Hartman

"You Got to Pay the Band" by Abbey Lincoln

"I Put a Spell on You" by Nina Simone

"Gimme a Pigfoot and a Bottle of Beer" by Billie Holiday

"Stormy Weather" by Lena Horne

"At Last" by Etta James

"Skylark" by Aretha Franklin

"Come Sunday!" by Kathleen Battle and Branford Marsalis

"Creole Love Call" by Kathleen Battle

"Autumn Leaves" by Wynton Marsalis and Sarah Vaughan

"La Belle Vie (The Good Life)" by Dee Dee Bridgewater

2. Spirituals

"My Lord What a Morning" by Florence Quivar

"Let Us Break Bread Together" by Jessye Norman

"Deep River" by Paul Robeson

"Were You There?" by Barbara Hendricks

"Joshua Fit the Battle of Jericho" by Mahalia Jackson

"Give Me Jesus" by Wayburn Dean

"Sweet Little Jesus Boy" by Leontyne Price

"God Bless the Child" by Gregory Porter

"Oh What a Beautiful City" by Marian Anderson

"Trouble of the World" by Mahalia
  Jackson
"Over My Head" by Kathleen Battle
"Wade in the Water" from Alvin Ailey's
  Revelations
"Didn't My Lord Deliver Daniel" from
  Alvin Ailey's *Revelations*
"There Is a Balm in Gilead" by Kathleen
  Battle and Jessye Norman
"A City Called Heaven" by Shirley Verrett

3. Gospel

"Abide with Me" by Thelonious Monk
"Blessed Assurance" by CeCe Winans and
  Terrence Blanchard
"His Eye on the Sparrow" by Lauren Hill
  and Tanya Blount
"Precious Lord (Take My Hand)" by
  Aretha Franklin
"I Love the Lord" by Whitney Houston
"Just a Closer Walk with Thee" by Louis
  Armstrong and Mahalia Jackson
"Amazing Grace" by Aretha Franklin
"I Love the Lord" by Jennifer Holliday
"Pass Me Not" by Fantasia Barrino
"A Quiet Place" by Take 6

"Stand" by Bebe Winans
"Lift Every Voice & Sing" by Committed
"How I Got Over" by Mahalia Jackson
"I Don't Feel No Ways Tired" by James
  Cleveland
"Jesus Loves Me" by Whitney Houston
"Near the Cross" by Rachelle Ferrell

4. Opera

George Gershwin's *Porgy and Bess* (cast
  recording with Alexander Smalls)
Kurt Wiell's *Lost in the Stars* (1949
  original Broadway cast with Todd
  Duncan)
Giacomo Puccini's *La bohème* (cast
  recording with Barbara Hendricks)
Wolfgang Amadeus Mozart's *Le nozze di
  Figaro* (cast recording with Kathleen
  Battle)
Georges Bizet's *Carmen* (cast recording
  with Jessye Norman)
Giuseppe Verdi's *Un ballo in maschera*
  (cast recording with Marian
  Anderson)
Giuseppe Verdi's *La traviata* (cast
  recording with Leontyne Price)

Giuseppe Verdi's *Aida* (cast recording
  with Leontyne Price)
Giacomo Puccini's *Turandot* (cast
  recording with Leontyne Price)
Henry Purcell's *Dido and Aeneas* (cast
  recording with Shirley Verrett)
Giuseppe Verdi's "O don fatale" aria from
  Don Carlo (cast recording with Grace
  Bumbry)
Giuseppe Verdi's *La forza del destino* (cast
  recording with Martina Arroyo)

5. Divas

"I'm Every Woman" by Whitney Houston
"Vissi d'arte" from *Tosca* performed by
  Leonytne Price
"Proud Mary" by Tina Tuner
"Formation" by Beyoncé
"O don fatale" from *Don Carlo* performed
  by Shirley Verrett
"Thy Hand, Belinda / When I Am Laid
  in Earth" from *Dido and Aeneas*
  performed by Jessye Norman
"And I am Telling You, I'm Not Going" by
  Jennifer Holliday
"Lady Marmalade" by Labelle

"My Man's Gone Now" from *Porgy and
  Bess* performed by Florence Quivar
"Un bel dì vedremo" from *Madama
  Butterfly* performed by Clamma Dale
"Come On-a My House" (live) by
  Eartha Kitt
"La Vie en rose" by Grace Jones
"Caro nome" from *Rigoletto* performed by
  Barbara Hendrix
"Ain't No Mountain High Enough" by
  Ashford & Simpson
"Una voce poco fa" from *Il barbiere di
  Siviglia* performed by Kathleen Battle
"Diamonds Are Forever" by Shirley
  Bassey
"Ave Maria" performed by Denyce
  Graves
"Upside Down" by Diana Ross

6. Jukebox Music

"I Got You (I Feel Good)" by
  James Brown
"(Your Love Keeps Lifting Me) Higher
  and Higher" by Jackie Wilson
"Mustang Sally" by Wilson Picket
"Try a Little Tenderness" by Otis Redding

"Rainy Night in Georgia" by Gladys
    Knight & the Pips
"People Get Ready" by The Impressions
"Hey Jude" by Wilson Pickett
"Papa Was a Rolling Stone" by the
    Temptations
"Let's Do It Again" by Curtis Mayfield
"Respect" by Aretha Franklin
"Let's Stay Together" by Al Green
"Be My Baby" by Ronnie Spector
"(Sittin' On) The Dock of the Bay" by Otis
    Redding
"When a Man Loves a Woman" by Percy
    Sledge
"Please Mr. Postman" by the Marvelettes
"Blueberry Hill" by Fats Domino
"Stand By Me" by the Drifters
"The Greatest Pretender" by the Platters

7. Serenades

"So Many Stars" by Kathleen Battle
"Bachianas brasileiras" by Heitor
    Villa-Lobos, performed by Barbara
    Hendricks
"Vocalise" by Sergei Rachmaninoff,
    performed by Leontyne Price

"A Song for You" by Donny Hathaway
"It's My Turn" by Aretha Franklin
"Somewhere in My Lifetime" by Phyllis
    Hyman
"Ave Maria" performed by Jessye Norman
"First Time Ever I Saw Your Face" by
    Roberta Flack
"Ain't No Way" by Aretha Franklin
"What a Difference a Day Makes" by
    Dinah Washington
"I've Been Loving You Too Long (to Stop
    Now)" by Etta James
"C'est si bon" by Eartha Kitt
"You Must Believe in Spring" by Cleo
    Laine
"I Can't Make You Love Me" by Nancy
    Wilson
"Romance" by Sarah Vaughan
"I (Who Have Nothing)" by Luther
    Vandross
"Black Butterfly" by Deniece Williams
"Unforgettable" by Nat King Cole
"Georgia on My Mind" by Ray Charles
"What's Going On" by Marvin Gaye

Index

Alexander's "Chase the Blues Away" Hot Dogs, 134–5

Allen, Debbie, 118

Anderson, Marian, 58

Angel Yeast Rolls, *172, 173*

Ashley, Clarence, 3

Baked Spicy Barbecue Beans, 90

Banana Pudding Custard Pie, 188–9

Battle, Kathleen, 6

Beard, James, 4

Birth of a Nation (movie), 132

biscuits

    Buttermilk, *159,* 160–1

    Jalapeño Cheddar, 168–9

    Jam, 164–5

    jukebox music's symbolic ties to, 6–7, 154, 156–7

    Sage Sausage, 7, 166–7

    Sweet Potato, 162–3

Blackberry Cobbler, 7, *194–5,* 194–6

black-eyed pea dishes

    Carolina Hoppin' John, 30, 34, *35*

    Field Greens, Poached Pear, and Black-Eyed Pea Salad, 2, 62–5, *63*

    Hoppin' John Cakes with Sweet Pepper Rémoulade, 22–4

Bourbon Barbecue Shrimp and Okra Skewers, 2, *15,* 16–7

Bourbon Chocolate Praline Truffles, 2, 7, *206–7,* 206–9

Bourbon Cream Sauce, 6, *120–1,* 121–3

Bourbon Pecan Pie, 185

Bourbon Praline Sauce, 146–8, *147*

Braised Oxtails, Turnips, and Okra, *151,* 152–3

bread. *See also specific bread categories*

    Angel Yeast Rolls, *172, 173*

    biscuits, 6–7, 156–7, *159,* 160–9

    corn, 11, *66,* 67–8, 136–7, 158

    desserts, 178–80, *181*

    jukebox music's symbolic ties to, 6–7, 154, 156–7

    muffins, 6–7, 156–8, 170, *171*

    symbolic cultural elements of, 6–7, 156–7

Broiled Sweet Corn with Tarragon-Cayenne Butter, *74,* 75

Buttermilk Biscuits, *159,* 160–1

Buttermilk Corn Bread Muffins, 158

Buttermilk Mac and Cheese, 11, *43,* 44–5

Cabbage, Pan-Fried, with Bacon, 97

Cabbage Slaw with Roasted Sweet Corn, *60,* 61

Caesar Dressing, Creole, 67–8

Café Beulah, 18, 22, 157

cakes. *See* desserts

Carolina Bourbon Barbecue Sauce, 2, *15,* 16–7

Carolina Bourbon Barbecue Shrimp and Okra Skewers, 2, *15,* 16–7

Carolina Cabbage Slaw with Roasted Sweet Corn, *60,* 61

Carolina Hoppin' John, 30, 34, *35*

Carolina Rice Pudding, *192,* 193

Catfish Corn Soup, 79

Catfish, Fried, 104, *105*

Charles, Ray, 190

Charleston Spicy Red Rice, 30, 36–7

Chase, Leah, 10

Chess Pie, 187

Chez Panisse restaurant, 7

chicken/fowl dishes

    divas' symbolic tie to, 6, 116, 118

    Free-Range Duck with Creole Sauce, 124–6, *125*

    Mustard-Barbecued Chicken Livers on Peppered Turnip Greens, 25–7

    Oven-Fried Baby Chickens with Hot Mustard-Apricot Jam Glaze, 127–9

    Roasted Stuffed Turkey with Corn Bread-Chestnut Dressing, 136–7

    Roast Quail in Bourbon Cream Sauce, 6, *120–1,* 121–3

    Savory Chicken Bog, *40–1,* 41–2

    Southern Fried Chicken Plate, 6, *131,* 132–3

Child, Julia, 4

Chili Slaw Dogs (Southern Hot Dogs), 134

Chocolate Pineapple Upside-Down Cake, 7, 202–3

Citrus-Glazed Pork Loin Roast with Corn Cream Sauce, 144–5

Citrus Vinaigrette, 2, 62–5, *63*

Citrus-Whipped Sweet Potatoes, 86

Cole, Nat King, 136, 176

Collard Greens with Smoked Turkey, *94,* 95–6

Corn Bread Canapé with Mustard-Barbecued Chicken Livers, 11

Corn Bread-Chestnut Dressing, 136–7

Corn Bread Croutons, *66,* 67–8

Corn Bread Muffins, Buttermilk, 158

Corn Catfish Soup with Bacon and Mint, 79

Corn Cream Sauce, 144–5

corn, cutting tips for, 77

Corn, Sweet, and Carolina Cabbage Slaw, *60,* 61

Corn, Sweet, with Tarragon-Cayenne Butter, *74,* 75

Crawfish Onion Gravy, 6, 148–9

Creole Caesar Salad with Corn Bread Croutons, *66,* 67–8

Creole Potato Salad, 83

Creole Sauce, 124–6, *125*

Croutons, Corn Bread, *66,* 67–8

Daisy (aunt), 48

Dash, Julie, 4

Daughters of the Dust (movie), 4

desserts

    Banana Pudding Custard Pie, 188–9

    Blackberry Cobbler, 7, *194–5,* 194–6

    Bourbon Chocolate Praline Truffles, 2, 7, *206–7,* 206–9

    Bourbon Pecan Pie, 185

    Carolina Rice Pudding, *192,* 193

    Chess Pie, 187

    Chocolate Pineapple Upside-Down Cake, 7, 202–3

    Doughnuts, 180, *181*

    Icebox Lemon Pie, 7, *182–3,* 183–4

    Pie Shell for, 186

    serenade music's symbolic tie to, 6–7, 174, 176–7

    Southern Comfort Peach Shortcake, 7, 200–1

Southern Pound Cake, *197,* 198–9

Sticky Buns, 178–9

Sweet Potato Coconut Cake, 204–5

Sweet Potato Pie, 190, *191*

Deviled Crab Cakes with Spicy Creole
    Mayonnaise, *18–9,* 18–21

Deviled Eggs, 11, *12–3,* 12–4

divas. *See also* chicken/fowl dishes; meat dishes
    foods symbolically tied to, 6, 116, 118
    music playlist for, 215

The Doctor of Alcantara (opera), 102

Doc Watson (Arthel Lane "Doc" Watson), 3

Doughnuts, 180, *181*

Duck with Creole Sauce, 124–6, *125*

Dunbar Pie: Macaroni with Meat Sauce, 46–7

The Ed Sullivan Show, 58

Eggs, Deviled, 11, 12, *12–3*

Fame (movie), 118

Field Greens, Poached Pear, and Black-Eyed
    Pea Salad with Citrus Vinaigrette,
    2, 62–5, *63*

Fitzgerald, Ella, 174

Franklin, Aretha, 119

Free-Range Duck with Creole Sauce, 124–6,
    125

Fresh Creamed Corn Garnished with Crispy
    Leeks, 77–8

Fried Catfish Plate, 104, *105*

Fried Okra, 67, 70, *71*

Fried Sweet White Corn, 76

Frogmore Stew, 110, *111*

Gates, Henry Louis, Jr., 103

Gaye, Marvin, 177

Gershwin, George, 102–3

Gershwin, Ira, 100, 102–3

The Gift of Southern Cooking (Lewis), 86

Giovanni, Nikki, 130

Glaze, Ginger-Berry, *141,* 142–3

Glaze, Hot Mustard-Apricot, 127–9

Glover, Danny, 52

gospel. *See also* greens/sides
    foods symbolically tied to, 6, 56, 58
    music playlist for, 214

gravy
    Crabmeat Pan, 32, *53,* 54–5
    Crawfish Onion, 6, 148–9
    Redeye, *138–9,* 139–40
    symbolic cultural elements of, 4–6, 32

Green Beans with Benne Seeds, 92, *93*

greens/sides
    Baked Spicy Barbecue Beans, 90
    Broiled Sweet Corn with Tarragon-Cayenne
      Butter, *74,* 75
    Carolina Cabbage Slaw with Roasted Sweet
      Corn, *60,* 61
    Citrus-Whipped Sweet Potatoes, 86
    Corn Catfish Soup with Bacon and
      Mint, 79
    Creole Caesar Salad with Corn Bread
      Croutons, *66,* 67–8
    Creole Potato Salad, 83
    Field Greens, Poached Pear, and Black-
      Eyed Pea Salad with Citrus Vinaigrette,
      2, 62–5, *63*

greens/sides (*continued*)
    Fresh Creamed Corn Garnished with Crispy
        Leeks, 77–8
    Fried Okra, 67, 70, *71*
    Fried Sweet White Corn, 76
    gospel's symbolic tie to, 6, 56, 58
    Herb-Sautéed Greens with Roasted Garlic
        and Turnips, 98–9
    Lady Lima Succotash Salad with Fresh Mint,
        11, *87,* 88–9
    Lemon Candied Yams, *84,* 85
    Pan-Fried Cabbage with Bacon, 97
    Roasted Okra with Herbs, Pepper, and
        Garlic, 73
    Sautéed Green Beans with Toasted
        Charleston Benne Seeds, 92, *93*
    Spicy Charleston Black Beans, 91
    Spicy Okra Shrimp Soup, 69
    Stewed Collard Greens with Smoked Turkey,
        94, 95–6
    Stewed Okra with Corn and Tomato, 72
    Sweet Pickle Potato Salad, 59, *80–1,* 80–2
Griffith, D. W., 132
grits
    with Sage Sausage Gravy, 32, 52
    Stone-Ground, 32, *50,* 51
    symbolic cultural elements of, 4–6, 31–2
Grouper with Gumbo Sauce, *106,* 107–8
Gullah Dirty Rice, 4, 30, 38–9
Gullah/Geechee culture, 4, 36, 75

Ham, Baked and Candied, 146–8, 147
Height, Dorothy, 3

Herb-Sautéed Greens with Roasted Garlic and
    Turnips, 98–9
the Hilltop House (club), 156
Holiday, Billie, 11
Hoppin' John Cakes with Sweet Pepper
    Rémoulade, 22–4
Hot Dogs, Alexander's, 134–5
Hot Mustard-Apricot Jam Glaze, 127–9

Icebox Lemon Pie, 7, 182–3, 183–4

Jackson, Mahalia, 58
Jalapeño Cheddar Biscuits, 168–9
Jam Biscuits, 164–5
James (uncle), 109
jazz. *See also* starter dishes
    elements of, 10–1
    foods symbolically tied to, 4, 8, 10–1
    music playlist for, 213
Jefferson, Thomas, 31
Joe (uncle), 149, 152, 156
Jones, Sissieretta, 102
Jordan, Louis, 102
jukeboxes. *See also* biscuits; bread; muffins
    foods symbolically tied to, 6–7, 154, 156–7
    music playlist for, 215–6

King Biscuit Hour (radio show), 2
"King Biscuit Stomp" (song), 3

Lady Lima Succotash Salad with Fresh Mint, 11,
    87, 88–9
"Lady Sings the Blues" (song), 11

Lemon Candied Yams, *84,* 85
Lewis, Edna, 7, 56, 86
Little Milton (James Milton Campbell, Jr.), 3
LuPone, Patti, 116

macaroni dishes, 4–6
    Buttermilk Mac and Cheese, 11, *43,* 44–5
    Dunbar Pie: Macaroni with Meat Sauce,
       46–7
    Macaroni Vegetable Salad, 48–9
Mae, Ruthie, 12
Marinated Venison Roast with Ginger-Berry
       Glaze, *141,* 142–3
Marsalis, Wynton, 8, 10
Mars, Bruno, 154
meat dishes
    Alexander's "Chase the Blues Away" Hot
       Dogs, 134–5
    Bourbon Praline Candied Baked Ham,
       146–8, *147*
    Braised Oxtails, Turnips, and Okra, *151,*
       152–3
    Citrus-Glazed Pork Loin Roast with Corn
       Cream Sauce, 144–5
    divas' symbolic tie to, 6, 116, 118
    Marinated Venison Roast with Ginger-Berry
       Glaze, *141,* 142–3
    Pan-Fried Rabbit with Root Vegetables and
       Redeye Gravy, *138–9,* 139–40
    Prime Rib Roast with Crawfish Onion Gravy,
       6, 148–9
Mildred (aunt), 109
Mitchell, Joni, 54

Ms. Means (author's grandfather's neighbor),
    198
muffins
    Buttermilk Corn Bread, 158
    jukebox music's symbolic tie to, 6–7, 154,
       156–7
    Sweet Potato, 7, 170, *171*
music playlists
    diva, 215
    gospel and hymns, 214
    jazz, 213
    jukebox, 215–6
    opera, 214–5
    serenades, 216
    spirituals, 213
Mustard-Barbecued Chicken Livers on
    Peppered Turnip Greens, 25–7
Mustard-Barbecued Sauce, 25–7

Norman, Jessye, 102

Okra and Shrimp Creole Sauté, 109
Okra and Shrimp Skewers, 2, *15,* 16–7
Okra, Fried, 67, 70, *71*
Okra, Roasted, 73
Okra Shrimp Spicy Soup, 69
Okra, Stewed, 72
Okra with Turnips and Oxtails, *151,*
    152–3
opera. *See also* seafood dishes
    food's symbolic ties to, 6, 100, 102–3
    historic, 102
    music playlist for, 214–5

Oven-Fried Baby Chickens with Hot Mustard-
    Apricot Jam Glaze, 127–9
Oxtails, Braised, *151,* 152–3

Pan-Fried Cabbage with Bacon, 97
Pan-Fried Rabbit with Root Vegetables and
    Redeye Gravy, *138–9,* 139–40
Parker, Charlie, 8
Pear, Poached, 2, 62–5, *63*
Pecan Bourbon Pie, 185
Pickles, Sweet, Potato Salad with, 59, *80–1,*
    80–2
pies. *See* desserts
Pineapple Chocolate Upside-Down Cake, 7,
    202–3
Porgy and Bess (opera), 102–3
Pork Loin Roast, 144–5
Potato Salad, Creole, 83
Potato Salad, Sweet Pickle, 59, *80–1,* 80–2
Praline Bourbon Candied Baked Ham,
    146–8, *147*
Praline Bourbon Chocolate Truffles, 2, 7,
    206–7, 206–9
Price, Leontyne, 6, 58, 102
Prime Rib Roast with Crawfish Onion Gravy,
    6, 148–9
Puccini, 6

Quail Roast, 6, *120–1,* 121–3
"Quilting the Black-Eyed Pea (We're Going to
    Mars)" (Giovanni), 130

Rabbit, Pan-Fried, *138–9,* 139–40
Redding, Otis, 119, 156
rice dishes
    Carolina Hoppin' John, 30, 34, *35*
    Carolina Rice Pudding, *192,* 193
    Charleston Spicy Red Rice, 30, 36–7
    Gullah Dirty Rice, 4, 30, 38–9
    Savory Chicken Bog, *40–1,* 41–2
    symbolic cultural elements of, 4–6, 30, 36
Roasted Okra with Herbs, Pepper, and
    Garlic, 73
Roasted Stuffed Turkey with Corn Bread-
    Chestnut Dressing, 136–7
Roast Quail in Bourbon Cream Sauce, 6, *120–1,*
    121–3
Roosevelt, Theodore, 102
Ross, Diana, 6

Sage Sausage Biscuits, 7, 166–7
Sage Sausage Gravy, 32, 52
salad
    Creole Caesar, *66,* 67–8
    Creole Potato, 83
    Field Greens, Poached Pear, and Black-Eyed
        Pea, 2, 62–5, *63*
    Lady Lima Succotash, 11, *87,* 88–9
    Macaroni Vegetable, 48–9
    Sweet Pickle Potato, 59, *80–1,* 80–2
sauce. *See also* gravy
    Bourbon Cream, 6, *120–1,* 121–3
    Bourbon Praline, 146–8, *147*
    Carolina Bourbon Barbecue, 2, *15,* 16

Corn Cream, 144–5

Creole, 124–6, *125*

Meat, 46–7

Mustard-Barbecue, 25–7

Spicy Gumbo, *106,* 107–8

Sautéed Green Beans with Toasted Charleston
    Benne Seeds, 92, *93*

Savory Chicken Bog, *40–1,* 41–2

seafood dishes

    Carolina Bourbon Barbecue Shrimp and
        Okra Skewers, 2, *15,* 16–7

    Corn Catfish Soup with Bacon and Mint, 79

    Deviled Crab Cakes with Spicy Creole
        Mayonnaise, *18–9,* 18–21

    Fried Catfish Plate, 104, *105*

    Frogmore Stew, 110, *111*

    opera's symbolic tie to, 6, 100, 102–3

    Seared Grouper with Spicy Gumbo Sauce,
        106, 107–8

    Sherry She-Crab Soup, *112,* 113–4, *115*

    Shrimp and Okra Creole Sauté, 109

    Smothered Shrimp and Crabmeat Pan Gravy,
        32, *53,* 54–5

    Spicy Okra Shrimp Soup, 69

serenades. *See also* desserts

    foods symbolically tied to, 6–7, 174, 176–7

    music playlist for, 216

sesame seeds, 92, *93*

Sherry She-Crab Soup, *112,* 113–4, *115*

Shoebox Café, 110, 157, 166

Shrimp and Okra Creole Sauté, 109

Shrimp and Okra Skewers, 2, *15,* 16–7

Shrimp Okra Spicy Soup, 69

Smithsonian Folkways Project, 2

Smothered Shrimp and Crabmeat Pan Gravy,
    32, *53,* 54–5

soup

    Catfish Corn with Bacon and Mint, 79

    Sherry She-Crab, *112,* 113–4, *115*

    Spicy Okra Shrimp, 69

South Carolina, 25, 36, 46

    Gullah/Geechee culture in, 4

    Low Country of, 22, 30, 72, 103, 113, 139

    peach industry in, 200

    rice industry in, 30

Southern Comfort Peach Shortcake, 7, 200–1

Southern Fried Chicken Plate, 6, *131,* 132–3

Southern Pound Cake, *197,* 198–9

Spicy Charleston Black Beans, 91

Spicy Creole Mayonnaise, *18–9,* 18–21

Spicy Gumbo Sauce, *106,* 107–8

Spicy Okra Shrimp Soup, 69

spirituals. *See also* grits; macaroni dishes; rice
    dishes

    foods symbolically tied to, 4–6, 30–2

    music playlist for, 213

starter dishes

    Carolina Bourbon Barbecue Shrimp and
        Okra Skewers, 2, *15,* 16–7

    Deviled Crab Cakes with Spicy Creole
        Mayonnaise, *18–9,* 18–21

    Deviled Eggs, 11, 12, *12–3*

    Hoppin John Cakes with Sweet Pepper
        Rémoulade, 22–4

starter dishes (*continued*)

    jazz's symbolic tie to, 4, 8, 10–1

    Mustard-Barbecued Chicken Livers on Peppered Turnip Greens, 25–7

Stewed Collard Greens with Smoked Turkey, *94,* 95–6

Stewed Okra with Corn and Tomato, 72

Sticky Buns, 178–9

Stone-Ground Grits, 32, *50,* 51

Succotash Salad, 11, *87,* 88–9

Sweet Pepper Rémoulade, 22–4

Sweet Pickle Potato Salad, 59, *80–1,* 80–2

Sweet Potato Biscuits, 162–3

Sweet Potato Coconut Cake, 204–5

Sweet Potatoes, Citrus-Whipped, 86

Sweet Potato Muffins, 7, 170, *171*

Sweet Potato Pie (recipe), 190, *191*

"Sweet Potato Pie" (song), 190

"Swing Low, Sweet Chariot" (song), 30

Symposium on American Cuisine, 36

to-go bags, 2, 206

Turkey, Roasted and Stuffed, 136–7

Turkey, Smoked, *94,* 95–6

Turner, Tina, 6, 118, 156

Turnip Greens and Chicken Livers, 25–7

Turnips and Sautéed Greens, 98–9

Turnips Braised with Okra and Oxtails, *151,* 152–3

Venison Roast, Marinated, *141,* 142–3

Washington Post, 36

Waters, Alice, 7

Watson, Doc, 3

West Africa, 2, 16, 132

    Gullah/Geechee descendents of, 4, 36

Williams, Big Joe, 3

Yams, Lemon Candied, 84, 85